THE COMMENTARIES OF CÆSAR

THE COMMENTARIES OF CÆSAR

ANTHONY TROLLOPE,
W. LUCAS COLLINS

ISBN: 978-93-89614-18-3

Published: 1870

LECTOR HOUSE LLP
E-MAIL: lectorpublishing@gmail.com

THE COMMENTARIES OF CÆSAR

BY

ANTHONY TROLLOPE

EDITED BY THE
REV. W. LUCAS COLLINS, M.A.

CONTENTS

CÆSAR

CHAPTER I.

INTRODUCTION.

It may perhaps be fairly said that the Commentaries of Cæsar are the beginning of modern history. He wrote, indeed, nearly two thousand years ago; but he wrote, not of times then long past, but of things which were done under his own eyes, and of his own deeds. And he wrote of countries with which we are familiar,—of our Britain, for instance, which he twice invaded, of peoples not so far remote but that we can identify them with our neighbours and ourselves; and he so wrote as to make us feel that we are reading actual history, and not romance. The simplicity of the narratives which he has left is their chief characteristic, if not their greatest charm. We feel sure that the circumstances which he tells us did occur, and that they occurred very nearly as he tells them. He deals with those great movements in Europe from which have sprung, and to which we can trace, the present political condition of the nations. Interested as the scholar, or the reader of general literature, may be in the great deeds of the heroes of Greece, and in the burning words of Greek orators, it is almost impossible for him to connect to any intimate and thoroughly-trusted link the fortunes of Athens, or Sparta, or Macedonia, with our own times and our own position. It is almost equally difficult to do so in regard to the events of Rome and the Roman power before the time of Cæsar. We cannot realise and bring home to ourselves the Punic Wars or the Social War, the Scipios and the Gracchi, or even the contest for power between Marius and Sulla, as we do the Gallic Wars and the invasion of Britain, by which the civilisation of Rome was first carried westwards, or the great civil wars,—the "Bellum Civile,"—by which was commenced a line of emperors continued almost down to our own days, and to which in some degree may be traced the origin and formation of almost every existing European nation. It is no doubt true that if we did but know the facts correctly, we could refer back every political and social condition of the present day to the remotest period of man's existence; but the interest fails us when the facts become doubtful, and when the mind begins to fear that history is mixed with romance. Herodotus is so mythic that what delight we have in his writings comes in a very slight degree from any desire on our part to form a continuous chain from the days of which he wrote down to our own. Between the marvels of Herodotus and the facts of Cæsar there is a great interval, from which have come down to us the works of various noble historians; but with

Cæsar it seems that that certainty commences which we would wish to regard as the distinguishing characteristic of modern history.

It must be remembered from the beginning that Cæsar wrote only of what he did or of what he caused to be done himself. At least he only so wrote in the two works of his which remain to us. We are told that he produced much besides his Commentaries,—among other works, a poem,—but the two Commentaries are all of his that we have. The former, in seven books, relates the facts of his seven first campaigns in Gaul for seven consecutive years; those campaigns in which he reduced the nations living between the Rhine, the Rhone, the Mediterranean, the Pyrenees, and the sea which we now call the British Channel.[1] The latter Commentary relates the circumstances of the civil war in which he contended for power against Pompey, his former colleague, with Crassus, in the first triumvirate, and established that empire to which Augustus succeeded after a second short-lived triumvirate between himself and Lepidus and Antony.

It is the object of this little volume to describe Cæsar's Commentaries for the aid of those who do not read Latin, and not to write Roman history; but it may be well to say something, in a few introductory lines, of the life and character of our author. We are all more or less familiar with the name of Julius Cæsar. In our early days we learned that he was the first of those twelve Roman emperors with whose names it was thought right to burden our young memories; and we were taught to understand that when he began to reign there ceased to exist that form of republican government in which two consuls elected annually did in truth preside over the fortunes of the empire. There had first been seven kings,—whose names have also been made familiar to us,—then the consuls, and after them the twelve Cæsars, of whom the great Julius was the first. So much we all know of him; and we know, too, that he was killed in the Capitol by conspirators just as he was going to become emperor, although this latter scrap of knowledge seems to be paradoxically at variance with the former. In addition to this we know that he was a great commander and conqueror and writer, who did things and wrote of them in the "veni, vidi, vici" style—saying of himself, "I came, I saw, I conquered." We know that a great Roman army was intrusted to him, and that he used this army for the purpose of establishing his own power in Rome by taking a portion of it over the Rubicon, which little river separated the province which he had been appointed to govern from the actual Roman territory within which, as a military servant of the magistrates of the republic, he had no business to appear as a general at the head of his army. So much we know; and in the following very short memoir of the great commander and historian, no effort shall be made,—as has been so frequently and so painfully done for us in late years,—to upset the teachings of our youth, and to prove that the old lessons were wrong. They were all fairly accurate, and shall now only be supplemented by a few further circumstances which were doubtless once learned by all school-boys and school-girls, but which some may perhaps have forgotten since those happy days.

Dean Merivale, in one of the early chapters of his admirable history of the

---

[1] There is an eighth book, referring to an eighth and ninth campaign, but it is not the work of Cæsar.

Romans under the Empire, declares that Caius Julius Cæsar is the greatest name in history. He makes the claim without reserve, and attaches to it no restriction, or suggestion that such is simply his own opinion. Claims of this nature, made by writers on behalf of their pet-heroes, we are, all of us, generally inclined to dispute; but this claim, great as it is, can hardly be disputed. Dr Merivale does not say that Cæsar was the greatest man that ever lived. In measuring such supremacy, men take for themselves various standards. To satisfy the judgment of one, it is necessary that a poet should be selected; for another, a teacher of religion; for a third, some intellectual hero who has assisted in discovering the secrets of nature by the operations of his own brain; for a fourth, a ruler,—and so on. But the names of some of these cannot be said to be great in history. Homer, Luther, Galileo, and Charles V., are great names,—as are also Shakespeare, Knox, Queen Elizabeth, and Newton. Among these, the two rulers would probably be the least in general admiration. But no one can assert that the names of the poets, divines, and philosophers, are greater than theirs in history. The Dean means that of all men who have lived, and whose deeds are known to us, Julius Cæsar did most to move the world; and we think that the Dean is right. Those whom we might, perhaps, compare with Cæsar, are Alexander, Charlemagne, Cromwell, Napoleon, and Washington. In regard to the first two, we feel, when claims are made for them, that they are grounded on the performance of deeds only partially known to us. In the days of Alexander, history was still dark,—and it had become dark again in those of Charlemagne. What Cromwell did was confined to our own islands, and, though he was great for us, he does not loom as large before the eyes of mankind in general as does one who moved all Europe, present and future. If there be any fair antagonist to Cæsar in this claim, it is Napoleon. As a soldier he was equally great, and the area of his operations was as extended. But there is an old saying which tells us that no one can be sure of his fortune till the end shall have come; and Cæsar's death on the steps of the Capitol was more in accordance with our ideas of greatness than that of Napoleon at St Helena. We cannot, moreover, but feel that there were fewer drawbacks from greatness in the personal demeanour of the Roman "Imperator" and Dictator than in that of the French Emperor. For Julius Cæsar was never really emperor, in that sense in which we use the word, and in accordance with which his successor Augustus really became an emperor. As to Washington, we may perhaps allow that in moral attributes he was the greatest of all. To aid his country he dared all,—even a rebel's disgraceful death, had he not succeeded where success was most improbable; and in all that he attempted he succeeded. His is the name that culminates among those of the men who made the United States a nation, and does so by the eager consent of all its people. And his work came altogether from patriotism,—with no alloy of personal ambition. But it cannot be said that the things he did were great as those which were done by Cæsar, or that he himself was as potent in the doing of them. He ventured everything with as grand a purpose as ever warmed the heart of man, and he was successful; but the things which he did were in themselves small in comparison with those effected by his less noble rival for fame. Mommsen, the German historian, describes Cæsar as a man too great for the scope of his intelligence and power of delineation. "The historian," he says, speaking of Cæsar, "when once in a thousand years he encounters the perfect, can only be silent regarding it." Napoleon also, in his life of Cæsar, paints his hero as perfect; but Napoleon when doing so is, in fact, claiming godlike perfection for that second Cæsar, his uncle. And the perfection which he claims is not that of which Mommsen speaks. The German intends to convey to us his conviction that Cæsar was perfect in human capacity and intelligence. Napoleon claims for him moral perfection. "We may be convinced," says the Emperor, "by the above facts, that during his first consulate, one only motive animated Cæsar,—namely, the public interest." We cannot, however, quite take the facts as the Emperor of the French gives them to us, nor can we share his conviction; but the common consent of reading men will probably acknowledge that there is in history no name so great as that of Julius Cæsar,—of whose written works some account is intended to be given in the following chapters.

He was born just one hundred years before Christ, and came of an old noble Roman family, of which Julius and not Cæsar was the distinctive name. Whence came the name of Cæsar has been a matter of doubt and of legend. Some say that it arose from the thick hair of one of the Julian tribe; others that a certain scion of the family, like Macduff, "was from his mother's womb untimely ripped," for which derivations Latin words are found to be opportune. Again we are told that one of the family once kept an elephant,—and we are referred to some eastern language in which the word for elephant has a sound like Cæsar. Another legend also rose from Cæsar's name, which, in the Gallic language of those days,—very luckily for Cæsar,—sounded as though one should say, "Send him back." Cæsar's horse once ran away with him, and carried him over to the enemy. An insolent Gaul, who knew him, called out, "Cæsar, Cæsar!" and so the other Gauls, obeying the order supposed to be given, allowed the illustrious one to escape. It must be acknowledged, however, that the learned German who tells us this story expresses a contemptuous conviction that it cannot be true. Whatever may have produced the word, its significance, derived from the doings and writings of Caius Julius, has been very great. It has come to mean in various languages the holder of despotic power; and though it is said that, as a fact, the Russian title Czar has no connection with the Roman word, so great is the prestige of the name, that in the minds of men the popular appellation of the Russian Emperor will always be connected with that of the line of the Roman Emperor.

Cæsar was the nephew by marriage of that Marius who, with alternations of bloody successes and seemingly irreparable ruin, had carried on a contest with Sulla for supreme power in the republic. Sulla in these struggles had represented the aristocrats and patricians,—what we perhaps may call the Conservative interest; while Marius, whose origin was low, who had been a common soldier, and, rising from the ranks, had become the darling of the army and of the people, may perhaps be regarded as one who would have called himself a Liberal, had any such term been known in those days. His liberality,—as has been the case with other political leaders since his time,—led him to personal power. He was seven times Consul, having secured his seventh election by atrocious barbarities and butcherings of his enemies in the city; and during this last consulship he died. The young Cæsar, though a patrician by birth, succeeded his uncle in the popular party, and seems from a very early age, — from his very boyhood, — to have looked forward to the power which he might win by playing his cards with discretion.

And very discreet he was, — self-confident to a wonderful degree, and patient also. It is to be presumed that most of our readers know how the Roman Republic fell, and the Roman Empire became established as the result of the civil wars which began with Marius and ended with, that "young Octavius" whom we better recognise as Augustus Cæsar. Julius Cæsar was the nephew by marriage of Marius, and Augustus was the great-nephew and heir of Julius. By means of conscriptions and murders, worse in their nature, though less probably in number, than those which disgraced the French Revolution, the power which Marius achieved almost without foresight, for which the great Cæsar strove from his youth upwards with constant foresight, was confirmed in the hands of Augustus, and bequeathed by him to the emperors. In looking back at the annals of the world, we shall generally find that despotic power has first grown out of popular movement against authority. It was so with our own Cromwell, has twice been so in the history of modern France, and certainly was so in the formation of the Roman Empire. In the great work of establishing that empire, it was the mind and hand and courage of Cæsar that brought about the result, whether it was for good or evil. And in looking at the lives of the three men — Marius, Cæsar, and Augustus, who followed each other, and all worked to the same end, the destruction of that oligarchy which was called a Republic in Rome — we find that the one was a man, while the others were beasts of prey. The cruelties of Marius as an old man, and of Augustus as a young one, were so astounding as, even at this distance, to horrify the reader, though he remembers that Christianity had not yet softened men's hearts. Marius, the old man, almost swam in the blood of his enemies, as also did his rival Sulla; but the young Octavius, he whom the gods favoured so long as the almost divine[2] Augustus, cemented his throne with the blood of his friends. To complete the satisfaction of Lepidus and Antony, his comrades in the second triumvirate, he did not scruple to add to the list of those who were to die, the names of the nearest and dearest to him. Between these monsters of cruelty — between Marius and Sulla, who went before him, and Octavius and Antony who followed him — Cæsar has become famous for clemency. And yet the hair of the reader almost stands on end with horror as Cæsar recounts in page after page the stories of cities burned to the ground, and whole communities slaughtered in cold blood. Of the destruction of the women and children of an entire tribe, Cæsar will leave the unimpassioned record in one line. But this at least may be said of Cæsar, that he took no delight in slaughter. When it became in his sight expedient that a people should suffer, so that others might learn to yield and to obey, he could give the order apparently without an effort. And we hear of no regrets, or of any remorse which followed the execution of it. But bloodshed in itself was not sweet to him. He was a discreet, far-seeing man, and could do without a scruple what discretion and caution demanded of him.

And it may be said of Cæsar that he was in some sort guided in his life by

---

[2] Cœlo tonantem credidimus Jovem
    Regnare; præsens Divus habebitur Augustus.

sense of duty and love of country; as it may also be said of his great contemporaries, Pompey and Cicero. With those who went before him, Marius and Sulla, as also with those who followed him, Antony and Augustus, it does not seem that any such motives actuated them. Love of power and greed, hatred of their enemies and personal ambition, a feeling that they were urged on by their fates to seek for high place, and a resolve that it was better to kill than be killed, impelled them to their courses. These feelings were strong, too, with Cæsar, as they are strong to this day with statesmen and with generals; but mingled with them in Cæsar's breast there was a noble idea, that he would be true to the greatness of Rome, and that he would grasp at power in order that the Roman Empire might be well governed. Augustus, doubtless, ruled well; and to Julius Cæsar very little scope for ruling was allowed after his battling was done; but to Augustus no higher praise can be assigned than that he had the intelligence to see that the temporary wellbeing of the citizens of Rome was the best guarantee for his own security.

Early in life Cæsar lifted himself to high position, though he did so in the midst of dangers. It was the wonder of those around him that Sulla did not murder him when he was young,—crush him while he was yet, as it were, in his shell; but Sulla spared him, and he rose apace. We are told that he became priest of Jupiter at seventeen, and he was then already a married man. He early trained himself as a public orator, and amidst every danger espoused the popular cause in Rome. He served his country in the East,—in Bithynia, probably,—escaping, by doing so, the perils of a residence in the city. He became Quæstor and then Ædile, assisted by all the Marian party, as that party would assist the rising man whom they regarded as their future leader. He attacked and was attacked, and was "indefatigable in harassing the aristocracy,"[3] who strove, but strove in vain, to crush him. Though young, and addicted to all the pleasures of youth,—a trifler, as Sulla once called him,—he omitted to learn nothing that was necessary for him to know as a chief of a great party and a leader of great armies. When he was thirty-seven he was made Pontifex Maximus, the official chief of the priesthood of Rome, the office greatest in honour of any in the city, although opposed by the whole weight of the aristocracy, and although Catulus was a candidate, who, of all that party, was the highest not only in renown but in virtue. He became Prætor the next year, though again he was opposed by all the influence of those who feared him. And, after his twelve months of office, he assumed the government of Spain,—the province allotted to him as Proprætor, in accordance with the usage of the Republic,—in the teeth of a decree of the Senate ordering him to remain in Rome. Here he gained his first great military success, first made himself known to his soldiery, and came back to Rome entitled to the honour of a triumph.

But there was still another step on the ladder of the State before he could assume the position which no doubt he already saw before him. He must be Consul before he could be the master of many legions, and in order that he might sue in proper form for the consulship, it was necessary that he should abandon his Triumph. He could only triumph as holding the office of General of the Republic's forces, and as General or Imperator he could not enter the city. He abandoned the

---

[3] The words are taken from Dean Merivale's history.

Triumph, sued for his office in the common fashion, and enabled the citizens to say that he preferred their service to his personal honours. At the age of forty-one he became Consul. It was during the struggle for the consulship that the triumvirate was formed, of which subsequent ages have heard so much, and of which Romans at the time heard probably so little. Pompey, who had been the political child of Sulla, and had been the hope of the patricians to whom he belonged, had returned to Rome after various victories which he had achieved as Proconsul in the East, had triumphed,—and had ventured to recline on his honours, disbanding his army and taking to himself the credit of subsiding into privacy. The times were too rough for such honest duty, and Pompey found himself for a while slighted by his party. Though he had thought himself able to abandon power, he could not bear the loss of it. It may be that he had conceived himself able to rule the city by his influence without the aid of his legions. Cæsar tempted him, and they two with Crassus, who was wanted for his wealth, formed the first triumvirate. By such pact among themselves they were to rule all Rome and all Rome's provinces; but doubtless, by resolves within himself of which no one knew, Cæsar intended even then to grasp the dominion of the whole in his own hands. During the years that followed,—the years in which Cæsar was engaged in his Gallic wars,—Pompey remained at Rome, not indeed as Cæsar's friend—for that hollow friendship was brought to an end by the death of Julia, Cæsar's daughter, whom Pompey, though five years Cæsar's elder, had married—but in undecided rivalship to the active man who in foreign wars was preparing legions by which to win the Empire. Afterwards, when Cæsar, as we shall hear, had crossed the Rubicon, their enmity was declared. It was natural that they should be enemies. In middle life, Pompey, as we have seen, had married Cæsar's daughter, and Cæsar's second wife had been a Pompeia.[4] But when they were young, and each was anxious to attach himself to the politics of his own party, Pompey had married the daughter-in-law of Sulla, and Cæsar had married the daughter of Cinna, who had almost been joined with Marius in leading the popular party. Such having been the connection they had made in their early lives, it was natural that Pompey and Cæsar should be enemies, and that the union of those two with any other third in a triumvirate should be but a hollow compromise, planned and carried out only that time might be gained.

Cæsar was now Consul, and from his consular chair laughed to scorn the Senate and the aristocratic colleague with whom he was joined,—Bibulus, of whom we shall again hear in the Commentary on the civil war. During his year of office

[4] She was that wife who was false with Clodius, and whom Cæsar divorced, declaring that Cæsar's wife must not even be suspected. He would not keep the false wife; neither would he at that moment take part in the accusation against Clodius, who was of his party, and against whom such accusation backed by Cæsar would have been fatal. The intrusion of the demagogue into Cæsar's house in the pursuit of Cæsar's wife during the mysteries of the Bona Dea became the subject of a trial in Rome. The offence was terrible and was notorious. Clodius, who was hated and feared by the patricians, was a favourite with the popular party. The offender was at last brought to trial, and was acquitted by venal judges. A word spoken by the injured husband would have insured his condemnation, but that word Cæsar would not speak. His wife he could divorce, but he would not jeopardise his power with his own party by demanding the punishment of him who had debauched her.

he seems to have ruled almost supreme and almost alone. The Senate was forced to do his bidding, and Pompey, at any rate for this year, was his ally. We already know that to prætors and to consuls, after their year of office in the city, were confided the government of the great provinces of the Republic, and that these officers while so governing were called proprætors and proconsuls. After his prætorship Cæsar had gone for a year to southern Spain, the province which had been assigned to him, whence he came back triumphant,—but not to enjoy his Triumph. At the expiration of his consulship the joint provinces of Cisalpine Gaul and Illyricum were assigned to him, not for one year, but for five years; and to these was added Transalpine Gaul, by which grant dominion was given to him over all that country which we now know as Northern Italy, over Illyria to the east, and to the west across the Alps, over the Roman province already established in the south of France. This province, bounded on the north by Lake Leman and the Swiss mountains, ran south, to the Mediterranean, and to the west half across the great neck of land which joins Spain to the continent of Europe. This province of Transalpine Gaul was already Roman, and to Cæsar was intrusted the task of defending this, and of defending Rome itself, from the terrible valour of the Gauls. That he might do this it was necessary that he should collect his legions in that other Gaul which we now know as the north of Italy.

It does not seem that there was any preconceived idea that Cæsar should reduce all Gallia beneath the Roman yoke. Hitherto Rome had feared the Gauls, and had been subject to their inroads. The Gauls in former years had even made their way as invaders into the very city, and had been bought out with a ransom. They had spread themselves over Northern Italy, and hence, when Northern Italy was conquered by Roman arms, it became a province under the name of Cisalpine Gaul. Then, during the hundred years which preceded Cæsar's wars, a province was gradually founded and extended in the south of France, of which Marseilles was the kernel. Massilia had been a colony of Greek merchants, and was supported by the alliance of Rome. Whither such alliance leads is known to all readers of history. The Greek colony became a Roman town, and the Roman province stretched itself around the town. It was Cæsar's duty, as governor of Transalpine Gaul, to see that the poor province was not hurt by those ravaging Gauls. How he performed that duty he tells us in his first Commentary.

During the fourth year of his office, while Pompey and Crassus, his colleagues in the then existing triumvirate, were consuls, his term of dominion over the three provinces was prolonged by the addition of five other years. But he did not see the end of the ten years in that scene of action. Julia, his daughter, had died, and his great rival was estranged from him. The Senate had clamoured for his recall, and Pompey, with doubtful words, had assented, A portion of his army was demanded from him, was sent by him into Italy in obedience to the Senate, and shortly afterwards was placed under the command of Pompey. Then Cæsar found that the Italian side of the Alps was the more convenient for his purposes, that the Hither or Cisalpine Gaul demanded his services, and that it would be well for him to be near the Rubicon. The second Commentary, in three books, 'De Bello Civili,' giving us his record of the civil war, tells us of his deeds and fortunes for the next two years,—the years B.C. 49 and 48. The continuation of his career as a general is related in three other Commentaries, not by his own hand, to which, as being beyond the scope of this volume, only short allusion will be made. Then came one year of power, full of glory, and, upon the whole, well used; and after that there came the end, of which the tale has been so often told, when he fell, stabbed by friend and foe, at the foot of Pompey's pillar in the Capitol.

It is only further necessary that a few words should be added as to the character of Cæsar's writings,—for it is of his writings rather than of his career that it is intended here to give some idea to those who have not an opportunity of reading them. Cæsar's story can hardly be told in this little volume, for it is the history of the world as the world then was. The word which our author has chosen as a name for his work,—and which now has become so well known as connected with Cæsar, that he who uses it seems to speak of Cæsar,—means, in Cæsar's sense, a Memoir. Were it not for Cæsar, a "Commentary" would be taken to signify that which the critic had added, rather than the work which the author had first produced. Cæsar's "Commentaries" are memoirs written by himself, descriptive of his different campaigns, in which he treats of himself in the third person, and tells his story as it might have been told by some accompanying scribe or secretary. This being so, we are of course driven to inquire whether some accompanying scribe or secretary may not in truth have done the work. And there is doubtless one great argument which must be powerful with us all towards the adoption of such a surmise. The amount of work which Cæsar had on hand, not only in regard to his campaigns, but in the conduct of his political career, was so great as to have overtasked any brain without the addition of literary labour. Surely no man was ever so worked; for the doctrine of the division of labour did not prevail then in great affairs as it does now. Cæsar was not only a general; he was also an engineer, an astronomer, an orator, a poet, a high priest—to whom, as such, though himself, as we are told, a disbeliever in the gods of Olympus, the intricate and complicated system of Roman worship was a necessary knowledge. And he was a politician, of whom it may be said that, though he was intimately acquainted with the ferocity of opposition, he knew nothing of its comparative leisure. We have had busy statesmen writing books, two prime ministers translating Homer, another writing novels, a fourth known as a historian, a dramatist, and a biographer. But they did not lead armies as well as the Houses of Parliament, and they were occasionally blessed by the opportunities of comparative political retirement which opposition affords. From the beginning of the Gallic war, Cæsar was fighting in person every year but one till he died. It was only by personal fighting that he could obtain success. The reader of the following pages will find that, with the solitary exception of the siege of Marseilles, nothing great was done for him in his absence. And he had to make his army as well as to lead it. Legion by legion, he had to collect it as he needed it, and to collect it by the force of his own character and of his own name. The abnormal plunder with which it was necessary that his soldiers should be allured to abnormal valour and toil had to be given as though from his own hand. For every detail of the soldiers' work he was responsible; and at the same time it was incumbent on him so to manipulate his Roman enemies at Rome,—and, harder still than that, his Roman friends,—that confusion and destruction should not fall upon him as a politician. Thus weighted, could he write his own Commentaries? There is reason to believe that there was collected by him, no doubt with the aid of his secretaries, a large body of notes which were known as the Ephemerides of Cæsar,—jottings down, as we may say, taken from day to day. Were not the Commentaries which bear Cæsar's name composed from these notes by some learned and cunning secretary?

These notes have been the cause of much scholastic wrath to some of the editors and critics. One learned German, hotly arguing that Cæsar wrote no Ephemerides, does allow that somebody must have written down the measurements of the journeys, of the mountains, and of the rivers, the numbers also of the captives and of the slaves.[5] "Not even I," says he,—"not even do I believe that Cæsar was able to keep all these things simply in his memory." Then he goes on to assert that to the keeping of such notes any scribe was equal; and that it was improbable that Cæsar could have found time for the keeping of notes when absolutely in his tent. The indignation and enthusiasm are comic, but the reasoning seems to be good. The notes were probably collected under Cæsar's immediate eyes by his secretaries; but there is ample evidence that the Commentaries themselves are Cæsar's own work. They seem to have become known at once to the learned Romans of the day; and Cicero, who was probably the most learned, and certainly the best critic of the time, speaks of them without any doubt as to their authorship. It was at once known that the first seven books of the Gallic War were written by Cæsar, and that the eighth was not. This seems to be conclusive. But in addition to this, there is internal evidence. Cæsar writes in the third person, and is very careful to maintain that mode of expression. But he is not so careful but that on three or four occasions he forgets himself, and speaks in the first person. No other writer, writing for Cæsar, would have done so. And there are certain trifles in the mode of telling the story, which must have been personal to the man. He writes of "young" Crassus, and "young" Brutus, as no scribe would have written; and he shows, first his own pride in obtaining a legion from Pompey's friendship, and then his unmeasured disgust when the Senate demand and obtain from him that legion and another one, and when Pompey uses them against himself, in a fashion which would go far to prove the authenticity of each Commentary, were any proof needed. But the assent of Cæsar's contemporaries suffices for this without other evidence.

And it seems that they were written as the wars were carried on, and that each was published at once. Had it not been so, we could not understand that Cæsar should have begun the second Commentary before he had finished the first. It seems that he was hindered by the urgency of the Civil War from writing what with him would have been the two last books of the Gallic War, and therefore put the completion of that work into the hands of his friend Hirtius, who wrote the memoir of the two years in one book. And Cæsar's mode of speaking of men who were at one time his friends and then his enemies, shows that his first Commentary was completed and out of hand before the other was written. Labienus, who in the Gallic War was Cæsar's most trusted lieutenant, went over to the other side and served under Pompey in the Civil War. He could not have failed to allude in

---

[5] Nipperdeius.

some way to the desertion of Labienus, in the first Commentary, had Labienus left him and joined Pompey while the first Commentary was still in his hands.

His style was at once recognised by the great literary critic of the day as being excellent for its intended purpose. Cæsar is manifestly not ambitious of literary distinction, but is very anxious to convey to his readers a narrative of his own doings, which shall be graphic, succinct, intelligible, and sufficiently well expressed to insure the attention of readers. Cicero, the great critic, thus speaks of the Commentaries; "Valde quidam, inquam, probandos; nudi enim sunt, recti, et venusti, omni ornatu orationis, tanquam veste, detracto." The passage is easily understood, but not perhaps very easily translated into English. "I pronounce them, indeed, to be very commendable, for they are simple, straightforward, agreeable, with all rhetorical ornament stripped from them, as a garment is stripped." This was written by Cicero while Cæsar was yet living, as the context shows. And Cicero does not mean to imply that Cæsar's writings are bald or uncouth: the word "venusti" is evidence of this. And again, speaking of Cæsar's language, Cicero says that Cæsar spoke with more finished choice of words than almost any other orator of the day. And if he so spoke, he certainly so wrote, for the great speeches of the Romans were all written compositions. Montaigne says of Cæsar: "I read this author with somewhat more reverence and respect than is usually allowed to human writings, one while considering him in his person, by his actions and miraculous greatness, and another in the purity and inimitable polish of his language and style, wherein he not only excels all other historians, as Cicero confesses, but peradventure even Cicero himself." Cicero, however, confesses nothing of the kind, and Montaigne is so far wrong. Cæsar was a great favourite with Montaigne, who always speaks of his hero with glowing enthusiasm.

To us who love to make our language clear by the number of words used, and who in writing rarely give ourselves time for condensation, the closely-packed style of Cæsar is at first somewhat difficult of comprehension. It cannot be read otherwise than slowly till the reader's mind is trained by practice to Cæsarean expressions, and then not with rapidity. Three or four adjectives, or more probably participles, joined to substantives in a sentence, are continually intended to convey an amount of information for which, with us, three or four other distinct sentences would be used. It is almost impossible to give the meaning of Cæsar in English without using thrice as many words as he uses. The same may be said of many Latin writers,—perhaps of all; so great was the Roman tendency to condensation, and so great is ours to dilution. But with Cæsar, though every word means much, there are often many words in the same sentence, and the reader is soon compelled to acknowledge that skipping is out of the question, and that quick reading is undesirable.

That which will most strike the ordinary English reader in the narrative of Cæsar is the cruelty of the Romans,—cruelty of which Cæsar himself is guilty to a frightful extent, and of which he never expresses horror. And yet among his contemporaries he achieved a character for clemency which he has retained to the present day. In describing the character of Cæsar, without reference to that of his contemporaries, it is impossible not to declare him to have been terribly cruel.

From bloodthirstiness he slaughtered none; but neither from tenderness did he spare any. All was done from policy; and when policy seemed to him to demand blood, he could, without a scruple,—as far as we can judge, without a pang,—order the destruction of human beings, having no regard to number, sex, age, innocence, or helplessness. Our only excuse for him is that he was a Roman, and that Romans were indifferent to blood. Suicide was with them the common mode of avoiding otherwise inevitable misfortune, and it was natural that men who made light of their own lives should also make light of the lives of others. Of all those with whose names the reader will become acquainted in the following pages, hardly one or two died in their beds. Cæsar and Pompey, the two great ones, were murdered. Dumnorix, the Æduan, was killed by Cæsar's orders. Vercingetorix, the gallantest of the Gauls, was kept alive for years that his death might grace Cæsar's Triumph. Ariovistus, the German, escaped from Cæsar, but we hear soon after of his death, and that the Germans resented it. He doubtless was killed by a Roman weapon. What became of the hunted Ambiorix we do not know, but his brother king Cativolcus poisoned himself with the juice of yew-tree. Crassus, the partner of Cæsar and Pompey in the first triumvirate, was killed by the Parthians. Young Crassus, the son, Cæsar's officer in Gaul, had himself killed by his own men that he might not fall into the hands of the Parthians, and his head was cut off and sent to his father. Labienus fell at Munda, in the last civil war in Spain. Quintus Cicero, Cæsar's lieutenant, and his greater brother, the orator, and his son, perished in the proscriptions of the second triumvirate. Titurius and Cotta were slaughtered with all their army by Ambiorix. Afranius was killed by Cæsar's soldiers after the last battle in Africa. Petreius was hacked to pieces in amicable contest by King Juba. Varro indeed lived to be an old man, and to write many books. Domitius, who defended Marseilles for Pompey, was killed in the flight after Pharsalia. Trebonius, who attacked Marseilles by land, was killed by a son-in-law of Cicero at Smyrna. Of Decimus Brutus, who attacked Marseilles by sea, one Camillus cut off the head and sent it as a present to Antony. Curio, who attempted to master the province of Africa on behalf of Cæsar, rushed amidst his enemy's swords and was slaughtered. King Juba, who conquered him, failing to kill himself, had himself killed by a slave. Attius Varus, who had held the province for Pompey, fell afterwards at Munda. Marc Antony, Cæsar's great lieutenant in the Pharsalian wars, stabbed himself. Cassius Longinus, another lieutenant under Cæsar, was drowned. Scipio, Pompey's partner in greatness at Pharsalia, destroyed himself in Africa. Bibulus, his chief admiral, pined to death. Young Ptolemy, to whom Pompey fled, was drowned in the Nile. The fate of his sister Cleopatra is known to all the world. Pharnaces, Cæsar's enemy in Asia, fell in battle. Cato destroyed himself at Utica. Pompey's eldest son, Cnæus, was caught wounded in Spain and slaughtered. Sextus the younger was killed some years afterwards by one of Antony's soldiers. Brutus and Cassius, the two great conspirators, both committed suicide. But of these two we hear little or nothing in the Commentaries; nor of Augustus Cæsar, who did contrive to live in spite of all the bloodshed through which he had waded to the throne. Among the whole number there are not above three, if so many, who died fairly fighting in battle.

The above is a list of the names of men of mark,—of warriors chiefly, of men who, with their eyes open, knowing what was before them, went out to encounter danger for certain purposes. The bloody catalogue is so complete, so nearly comprises all whose names are mentioned, that it strikes the reader with almost a comic horror. But when we come to the slaughter of whole towns, the devastation of country effected purposely that men and women might starve, to the abandonment of the old, the young, and the tender, that they might perish on the hillsides, to the mutilation of crowds of men, to the burning of cities told us in a passing word, to the drowning of many thousands,—mentioned as we should mention the destruction of a brood of rats,—the comedy is all over, and the heart becomes sick. Then it is that we remember that the coming of Christ has changed all things, and that men now,—though terrible things have been done since Christ came to us,—are not as men were in the days of Cæsar.

CHAPTER II.

First Book Of The War In Gaul.—Cæsar Drives First The Swiss And Then The Germans Out Of Gaul.—B.C. 58.

It has been remarked in the preceding chapter that Cæsar does not appear to have received any commission for the subjugation of Gaul when he took military charge of his three provinces. The Gauls were still feared in Rome, and it was his duty to see that they did not make their way over the Alps into the Roman territory. It was also his duty to protect from invasion, and also from rebellion, that portion of Gaul which had already been constituted a Roman province, but in which the sympathies of the people were still rather with their old brethren than with their new masters. The experience, however, which we have of great and encroaching empires tells us how probable it is that the protection of that which the strong already holds should lead to the grasping of more, till at last all has been grasped. It is thus that our own empire in India has grown. It was thus that the Spanish empire grew in America. It is thus that the empire of the United States is now growing. It was thus that Prussia, driven, as we all remember, by the necessity of self-preservation, took Nassau the other day, and Hanover and Holstein and Hesse. It was thus that the wolf claimed all the river, not being able to endure the encroaching lamb. The humane reader of history execrates, as he reads, the cruel, all-absorbing, ravenous wolf. But the philosophical reader perceives that in this way, and in no other, is civilisation carried into distant lands. The wolf, though he be a ravenous wolf, brings with him energy and knowledge.

What may have been Cæsar's own aspirations in regard to Gaul, when the government of the provinces was confided to him, we have no means of knowing. We may surmise,—indeed we feel that we know,—that he had a project in hand much greater to him, in his view of its result, than could be the adding of any new province to the Republic, let the territory added be as wide as all Gaul. He had seen enough of Roman politics to know that real power in Rome could only belong to a master of legions. Both Marius and Sulla had prevailed in the city by means of the armies which they had levied as the trusted generals of the Republic. Pompey had had his army trained to conquest in the East, and it had been expected that he also would use it to the same end. He had been magnanimous, or half-hearted, or imprudent, as critics of his conduct might choose to judge him then and may choose to judge him now, and on reaching Italy from the East had disbanded his legions. As a consequence, he was at that moment, when Cæsar was looking out into the future and preparing his own career, fain to seek some influence in the city by joining himself in a secret compact with Cæsar, his natural enemy, and with

Crassus. Cæsar, seeing all this, knowing how Marius and Sulla had succeeded and had failed, seeing what had come of the magnanimity of Pompey—resolved no doubt that, whatever might be the wars in which they should be trained, he would have trained legions at his command. When, therefore, he first found a cause for war, he was ready for war. He had not been long proconsul before there came a wicked lamb and drank at his stream.

In describing to us the way in which he conquered lamb after lamb throughout the whole country which he calls Gallia, he tells us almost nothing of himself. Of his own political ideas, of his own ambition, even of his doings in Italy through those winter months which he generally passed on the Roman side of the Alps, having left his army in winter quarters under his lieutenants, he says but a very few words. His record is simply the record of the campaigns; and although he now and then speaks of the dignity of the Republic, he hardly ever so far digresses from the narrative as to give to the reader any idea of the motives by which he is actuated. Once in these seven memoirs of seven years' battling in Gaul, and once only, does he refer to a motive absolutely personal to himself. When he succeeded in slaughtering a fourth of the emigrating Swiss, which was his first military success in Gaul, he tells us that he had then revenged an injury to himself as well as an injury to the Republic, because the grandfather of his father-in-law had in former wars been killed by the very tribe which he had just destroyed!

It is to be observed, also, that he does not intentionally speak in the first person, and that when he does so it is in some passage of no moment, in which the personality is accidental and altogether trivial. He does not speak of "I" and "me," but of Cæsar, as though he, Cæsar, who wrote the Commentary, were not the Cæsar of whom he is writing. Not unfrequently he speaks strongly in praise of himself; but as there is no humility in his tone, so also is there no pride, even when he praises himself. He never seems to boast, though he tells us of his own exploits as he does of those of his generals and centurions. Without any diffidence he informs us now and again how, at the end of this or that campaign, a "supplication," or public festival and thanksgiving for his victories, was decreed in Rome, on the hearing of the news,—to last for fifteen or twenty days, as the case might be.

Of his difficulties at home,—the political difficulties with which he had to contend,—he says never a word. And yet at times they must have been very harassing. We hear from other sources that during these wars in Gaul his conduct was violently reprobated in Rome, in that he had, with the utmost cruelty, attacked and crushed states supposed to be in amity with Rome, and that it was once even proposed to give him up to the enemy as a punishment for grievous treachery to the enemy. Had it been so resolved by the Roman Senate,—had such a law been enacted,—the power to carry out the law would have been wanted. It was easier to grant a "supplication" for twenty days than to stop his career after his legions had come to know him.

Nor is there very much said by Cæsar of his strategic difficulties; though now and then, especially when his ships are being knocked about on the British coast, and again when the iron of his heel has so bruised the Gauls that they all turn against him in one body under Vercingetorix, the reader is allowed to see that he is pressed hard enough. But it is his rule to tell the thing he means to do, the way he does it, and the completeness of the result, in the fewest possible words. If any student of the literature of battles would read first Cæsar's seven books of the Gallic War, and then Mr Kinglake's first four volumes of the 'Invasion of the Crimea,' he would be able to compare two most wonderful examples of the dexterous use of words, in the former of which the narrative is told with the utmost possible brevity, and in the latter with almost the utmost possible prolixity. And yet each narrative is equally clear, and each equally distinguished by so excellent an arrangement of words, that the reader is forced to acknowledge that the story is told to him by a great master.

In praising others,—his lieutenants, his soldiers, and occasionally his enemies,—Cæsar is often enthusiastic, though the praise is conferred by a word or two,—is given, perhaps, simply in an epithet added on for that purpose to a sentence planned with a wholly different purpose. Of blame he is very sparing; so much so, that it almost seems that he looked upon certain imperfections, in regard even to faith as well as valour or prudence, as necessary to humanity, and pardonable because of their necessity. He can tell of the absolute destruction of a legion through the folly and perhaps cowardice of one of his lieutenants, without heaping a word of reproach on the name of the unfortunate. He can relate how a much-favoured tribe fell off from their faith again and again without expressing anger at their faithlessness, and can explain how they were,—hardly forgiven, but received again as friends,—because it suited him so to treat them. But again he can tell us, without apparently a quiver of the pen, how he could devote to destruction a city with all its women and all its children, so that other cities might know what would come to them if they did not yield and obey, and become vassals to the godlike hero in whose hands Providence had placed their lives and their possessions.

It appears that Cæsar never failed to believe in himself. He is far too simple in his language, and too conscious of his own personal dignity, to assert that he has never been worsted. But his very simplicity seems to convey the assurance that such cannot ultimately be the result of any campaign in which he is engaged. He seems to imply that victory attends him so certainly that it would be futile in any case to discuss its probability. He feared no one, and was therefore the cause of awe to others. He could face his own legions when they would not obey his call to arms, and reduce them to obedience by a word. Lucan, understanding his character well, says of him that "he deserved to be feared, for he feared nothing;" "meruitque timeri Nil metuens." He writes of himself as we might imagine some god would write who knew that his divine purpose must of course prevail, and who would therefore never be in the way of entertaining a doubt. With Cæsar there is always this godlike simplicity, which makes his "Veni, vidi, vici," the natural expression of his mind as to his own mode of action. The same thing is felt in the very numerous but very brief records of the punishments which he inflicted. Cities are left desolate, as it were with a wave of his hand, but he hardly deigns to say that his own hand has even been waved. He tells us of one Acco who had opposed him, that, "Graviore sententiâ pronunciatâ,"—as though there had been some jury to pronounce this severe sentence, which was in fact pronounced only by himself,

Cæsar,—he inflicted punishment on him "more majorum." We learn from other sources that this punishment consisted in being stripped naked, confined by the neck in a cleft stick, and then being flogged to death. In the next words, having told us in half a sentence that he had made the country too hot to hold the fugitive accomplices of the tortured chief, he passes on into Italy with the majestic step of one much too great to dwell long on these small but disagreeable details. And we feel that he is too great.

It has been already said that the great proconsular wolf was not long in hearing that a lamb had come down to drink of his stream. The Helvetii, or Swiss, as we call them,—those tribes which lived on the Lake Leman, and among the hills and valleys to the north of the lake,—had made up their minds that they were inhabiting but a poor sort of country, and that they might considerably better themselves by leaving their mountains and going out into some part of Gaul, in which they might find themselves stronger than the existing tribes, and might take possession of the fat of the land. In doing so, their easiest way out of their own country would lie by the Rhone, where it now runs through Geneva into France. But in taking this route the Swiss would be obliged to pass over a corner of the Roman province. Here was a case of the lamb troubling the waters with a vengeance. When this was told to Cæsar,—that these Swiss intended, "facero iter per Provinciam nostram"—"to do their travelling through our Province,"—he hurried over the Alps into Gaul, and came to Geneva as fast as he could travel.

He begins his first book by a geographical definition of Gaul, which no doubt was hardly accurate, but which gives us a singularly clear idea of that which Cæsar desired to convey. In speaking of Gallia he intends to signify the whole country from the outflow of the Rhine into the ocean down to the Pyrenees, and then eastward to the Rhone, to the Swiss mountains, and the borders of the Roman Province. This he divides into three parts, telling us that the Belgians inhabited the part north of the Seine and Marne, the people of Aquitania the part south of the Garonne, and the Gauls or Celts the intermediate territory. Having so far described the scene of his action, he rushes off at once to the dreadful sin of the Swiss emigrants in desiring to pass through "our Province."

He has but one legion in Further Gaul,—that is, in the Roman province on the further side of the Alps from Rome; and therefore, when ambassadors come to him from the Swiss, asking permission to go through the corner of land, and promising that they will do no harm in their passage, he temporises with them. He can't give them an answer just then, but must think of it. They must come back to him by a certain day,—when he will have more soldiers ready. Of course he refuses. The Swiss make some slight attempt, but soon give that matter up in despair. There is another way by which they can get out of their mountains,—through the territory of a people called Sequani; and for doing this they obtain leave. But Cæsar knows how injurious the Swiss lambs will be to him and his wolves, should they succeed in getting round to the back of his Province,—that Roman Province which left the name of Provence in modern France till France refused to be divided any longer into provinces. And he is, moreover, invited by certain friends of the Roman Republic, called the Ædui, to come and stop these rough Swiss travellers.

He is always willing to help the Ædui, although these Ædui are a fickle, inconstant people,—and he is, above all things, willing to get to war. So he comes upon the rear of the Swiss when three portions of the people have passed the river Arar (Saone), and one portion is still behind. This hindermost tribe,—for the wretches were all of one tribe or mountain canton,—he sets upon and utterly destroys; and on this occasion congratulates himself on having avenged himself upon the slayers of the grandfather of his father-in-law.

There can be nothing more remarkable in history than this story of the attempted emigration of the Helvetii, which Cæsar tells us without the expression of any wonder. The whole people made up their minds that, as their borders were narrow, their numbers increasing, and their courage good, they would go forth,—men, women, and children,—and seek other homes. We read constantly of the emigrations of people,—of the Northmen from the north covering the southern plains, of Danes and Jutes entering Britain, of men from Scandinavia coming down across the Rhine, and the like. We know that after this fashion the world has become peopled. But we picture to ourselves generally a concourse of warriors going forth and leaving behind them homes and friends, to whom they may or may not return. With these Swiss wanderers there was to be no return. All that they could not take with them they destroyed, burning their houses, and burning even their corn, so that there should be no means of turning their steps backward. They do make considerable progress, getting as far into France as Autun,—three-fourths of them at least getting so far; but near this they are brought to an engagement by Cæsar, who outgenerals them on a hill. The prestige of the Romans had not as yet established itself in these parts, and the Swiss nearly have the best of it. Cæsar owns, as he does not own again above once or twice, that the battle between them was very long, and for long very doubtful. But at last the poor Helvetii are driven in slaughter. Cæsar, however, is not content that they should simply fly. He forces them back upon their old territory,—upon their burnt houses and devastated fields,—lest certain Germans should come and live there, and make themselves disagreeable. And they go back;—so many, at least, go back as are not slain in the adventure. With great attempt at accuracy, Cæsar tells us that 368,000 human beings went out on the expedition, and that 110,000, or less than a third, found their way back. Of those that perished, many hecatombs had been offered up to the shade of his father-in-law's grandfather.

Hereupon the Gauls begin to see how great a man is Cæsar. He tells us that no sooner was that war with the Swiss finished than nearly all the tribes of Gallia send to congratulate him. And one special tribe, those Ædui,—of whom we hear a great deal, and whom we never like because they are thoroughly anti-Gallican in all their doings till they think that Cæsar is really in trouble, and then they turn upon him,—have to beg of him a great favour. Two tribes,—the Ædui, whose name seems to have left no trace in France, and the Arverni, whom we still know in Auvergne,—have been long contending for the upper hand; whereupon the Arverni and their friends the Sequani have called in the assistance of certain Germans from across the Rhine. It went badly then with the Ædui. And now one of their kings, named Divitiacus, implores the help of Cæsar. Would Cæsar be kind enough to expel these horrid Germans, and get back the hostages, and free them from a burdensome dominion, and put things a little to rights? And, indeed, not only were the Ædui suffering from these Germans, and their king, Ariovistus; it is going still worse with the Sequani, who had called them in. In fact, Ariovistus was an intolerable nuisance to that eastern portion of Gaul. Would Cæsar be kind enough to drive him out? Cæsar consents, and then we are made to think of another little fable, — of the prayer which the horse made to the man for assistance in his contest with the stag, and of the manner in which the man got upon the horse, and never got down again. Cæsar was not slow to mount, and when once in the saddle, certainly did not mean to leave it.

Cæsar tells us his reasons for undertaking this commission. The Ædui had often been called "brothers" and "cousins" by the Roman Senate; and it was not fitting that men who had been so honoured should be domineered over by Germans. And then, unless these marauding Germans could be stopped, they would fall into the habit of coming across the Rhine, and at last might get into the Province, and by that route into Italy itself. And Ariovistus himself was personally so arrogant a man that the thing must be made to cease. So Cæsar sends ambassadors to Ariovistus, and invites the barbarian to a meeting. The barbarian will not come to the meeting. If he wanted to see the Roman, he would go to the Roman: if the Roman wants to see him, the Roman may come to him. Such is the reply of Ariovistus. Ambassadors pass between them, and there is a good deal of argument, in which the barbarian has the best of it. Cæsar, with his godlike simplicity, scorns not to give the barbarian the benefit of his logic. Ariovistus reminds Cæsar that the Romans have been in the habit of governing the tribes conquered by them after their fashion, without interference from him, Ariovistus; and that the Germans claim and mean to exercise the same right. He goes on to say that he is willing enough to live in amity with the Romans; but will Cæsar be kind enough to remember that the Germans are a people unconquered in war, trained to the use of arms, and how hardy he might judge when he was told that for fourteen years they had not slept under a roof? In the mean time other Gauls were complaining, and begging for assistance. The Treviri, people of the country where Treves now stands, are being harassed by the terrible yellow-haired Suevi, who at this time seem to have possessed nearly the whole of Prussia as it now exists on the further side of the Rhine, and who had the same desire to come westward that the Prussians have evinced since. And a people called the Harudes, from the Danube, are also harassing the poor Ædui. Cæsar, looking at these things, sees that unless he is quick, the northern and southern Germans may join their forces. He gets together his commissariat, and flies at Ariovistus very quickly.

Throughout all his campaigns, Cæsar, as did Napoleon afterwards, effected everything by celerity. He preaches to us no sermon on the subject, favours us with no disquisition as to the value of despatch in war, but constantly tells us that he moved all his army "magnis itineribus" — by very rapid marches; that he went on with his work night and day, and took precautions "magno opere," — with much labour and all his care, — to be beforehand with the enemy. In this instance Ariovistus tries to reach a certain town of the poor Sequani, then called Vesontio, now known to us as Besançon,—the same name, but very much altered. It consisted of a hill, or natural fortress, almost surrounded by a river, or natural fosse. There is nothing, says Cæsar, so useful in a war as the possession of a place thus naturally strong. Therefore he hurries on and gets before Ariovistus, and occupies the town. The reader already begins to feel that Cæsar is destined to divine success. The reader indeed knows that beforehand, and expects nothing worse for Cæsar than hairbreadth escapes. But the Romans themselves had not as yet the same confidence in him. Tidings are brought to him at Vesontio that his men are terribly afraid of the Germans. And so, no doubt, they were. These Romans, though by the art of war they had been made fine soldiers,—though they had been trained in the Eastern conquests and the Punic wars, and invasions of all nations around them,— were nevertheless, up to this day, greatly afraid even of the Gauls. The coming of the Gauls into Italy had been a source of terror to them ever since the days of Brennus. And the Germans were worse than the Gauls. The boast made by Ariovistus that his men never slept beneath a roof was not vain or useless. They were a horrid, hirsute, yellow-haired people, the flashing aspect of whose eyes could hardly be endured by an Italian. The fear is so great that the soldiers "sometimes could not refrain even from tears;"—"neque interdum lacrimas tenere poterant." When we remember what these men became after they had been a while with Cæsar, their blubbering awe of the Germans strikes us as almost comic. And we are reminded that the Italians of those days were, as they are now, more prone to show the outward signs of emotion than is thought to be decorous with men in more northern climes. We can hardly realise the idea of soldiers crying from fear. Cæsar is told by his centurions that so great is this feeling, that the men will probably refuse to take up their arms when called upon to go out and fight; whereupon he makes a speech to all his captains and lieutenants, full of boasting, full of scorn, full, no doubt, of falsehood, but using a bit of truth whenever the truth could aid him. We know that among other great gifts Cæsar had the gift of persuasion. From his tongue, also, as from Nestor's, could flow "words sweeter than honey,"—or sharper than steel. At any rate, if others will not follow him, his tenth legion, he knows, will be true to him. He will go forth with that one legion,—if necessary, with that legion of true soldiers, and with no others. Though he had been at his work but a short time, he already had his picked men, his guards, his favourite regiments, his tenth legion; and he knew well how to use their superiority and valour for the creation of those virtues in others.

Then Ariovistus sends ambassadors, and declares that he now is willing to meet Cæsar. Let them meet on a certain plain, each bringing only his cavalry guard. Ariovistus suggests that foot-soldiers might be dangerous, knowing that Cæsar's foot-soldiers would be Romans, and that his cavalry are Gauls. Cæsar agrees, but takes men out of his own tenth legion, mounted on the horses of the less-trusted allies. The accounts of these meetings, and the arguments which we are told are used on this and that side, are very interesting. We are bound to remember that Cæsar is telling the story for both sides, but we feel that he tries to tell it fairly. Ariovistus had very little to say to Cæsar's demands, but a great deal to say about his own exploits. The meeting, however, was broken up by an attack made by the Germans on Cæsar's mounted guard, and Cæsar retires,—not, however, before he has explained to Ariovistus his grand idea of the protection due by Rome to her allies. Then Ariovistus proposes another meeting, which Cæsar declines to attend, sending, however, certain ambassadors. Ariovistus at once throws the ambassadors into chains, and then there is nothing for it but a fight.

The details of all these battles cannot be given within our short limits, and there is nothing special in this battle to tempt us to dwell upon it. Cæsar describes to us the way in which the German cavalry and infantry fought together, the footmen advancing from amidst the horsemen, and then returning for protection. His own men fight well, and the Germans, in spite of their flashing eyes, are driven headlong in a rout back to the Rhine. Ariovistus succeeds in getting over the river and saving himself, but he has to leave his two daughters behind, and his two wives. The two wives and one of the daughters are killed; the other daughter is taken prisoner. Cæsar had sent as one of his ambassadors to the German a certain dear friend of his, who, as we heard before, was, with his comrade, at once subjected to chains. In the flight this ambassador is recovered. "Which thing, indeed, gave Cæsar not less satisfaction than the victory itself,—in that he saw one of the honestest men of the Province of Gaul, his own familiar friend and guest, rescued from the hands of his enemies and restored to him. Nor did Fortune diminish this gratification by any calamity inflicted on the man. Thrice, as he himself told the tale, had it been decided by lot in his own presence whether he should then be burned alive or reserved for another time." So Cæsar tells the story, and we like him for his enthusiasm, and are glad to hear that the comrade ambassador also is brought back.

The yellow-haired Suevi, when they hear of all this, desist from their invasion on the lower Rhine, and hurry back into their own country, not without misfortunes on the road. So great already is Cæsar's name, that tribes, acting as it were on his side, dare to attack even the Suevi. Then, in his "Veni, vidi, vici" style, he tells us that, having in one summer finished off two wars, he is able to put his army into winter quarters even before the necessary time, so that he himself may go into his other Gaul across the Alps,—"ad conventus agendos,"—to hold some kind of session or assizes for the government of his province, and especially to collect more soldiers.

CHAPTER III.

Second Book Of The War In Gaul.—Cæsar Subdues The Belgian Tribes.—B.C. 57.

The man had got on the horse's back, but the horse had various disagreeable enemies in attacking whom the man might be very useful, and the horse was therefore not as yet anxious to unseat his rider. Would Cæsar be so good as to go and conquer the Belgian tribes? Cæsar is not slow in finding reasons for so doing. The Belgians are conspiring together against him. They think that as all Gaul has been reduced,—or "pacified," as Cæsar calls it,—the Roman conqueror will certainly bring his valour to bear upon them, and that they had better be ready. Cæsar suggests that it would no doubt be felt by them as a great grievance that a Roman army should remain all the winter so near to them. In this way, and governed by these considerations, the Belgian lambs disturb the stream very sadly, and the wolf has to look to it. He collects two more legions, and, as soon as the earth brings forth the food necessary for his increased number of men and horses, he hurries off against these Belgian tribes of Northern Gallia. Of these, one tribe, the Remi, immediately send word to him that they are not wicked lambs like the others; they have not touched the waters. All the other Belgians, say the Remi, and with them a parcel of Germans, are in a conspiracy together. Even their very next-door neighbours, their brothers and cousins, the Suessiones, are wicked; but they, the Remi, have steadily refused even to sniff at the stream, which they acknowledge to be the exclusive property of the good wolf. Would the wolf be kind enough to come and take possession of them and all their belongings, and allow them to be the humblest of his friends? We come to hate these Remi, as we do the Ædui; but they are wise in their generation, and escape much of the starvation and massacring and utter ruin to which the other tribes are subjected. Among almost all these so-called Belgian tribes we find the modern names which are familiar to us. Rheims is in the old country of the Remi, Soissons in that of the Suessiones. Beauvais represents the Bellovaci, Amiens the Ambiani, Arras the Atrebates, Treves the Treviri,—as has been pointed out before. Silva Arduenna is, of course, the Forest of Ardennes.

The campaign is commenced by an attack made by the other Belgians on those unnatural Remi who have gone over to the Romans. There is a town of theirs, Bibrax, now known, or rather not known, as Bievre, and here the Remi are besieged by their brethren. When Bibrax is on the point of falling,—and we can imagine what would then have been the condition of the townsmen,—they send to Cæsar, who is only eight miles distant. Unless Cæsar will help, they cannot endure any longer such onslaught as is made on them. Cæsar, having bided his time, of course sends help, and the poor besieging Belgians fall into inextricable confusion. They agree to go home, each to his own country, and from thence to proceed to the defence of any tribe which Cæsar might attack. "So," says Cæsar, as he ends the story of this little affair, "without any danger on our part, our men killed as great a number of theirs as the space of the day would admit." When the sun set, and not till then, came an end to the killing, — such having been the order of Cæsar.

That these Belgians had really formed any intention of attacking the Roman province, or even any Roman ally, there is no other proof than that Cæsar tells us that they had all conspired. But whatever might be their sin, or what the lack of sin on their part, he is determined to go on with the war till he has subjugated them altogether. On the very next day he attacks the Suessiones, and gets as far as Noviodunum, — Noyons. The people there, when they see how terrible are his engines of war, give up all idea of defending themselves, and ask for terms. The Bellovaci do the same. At the instigation of his friends the Remi, he spares the one city, and, to please the Ædui, the other. But he takes away all their arms, and exacts hostages. From the Bellovaci, because they have a name as a powerful people, he takes 600 hostages. Throughout all these wars it becomes a matter of wonder to us what Cæsar did with all these hostages, and how he maintained them. It was, however, no doubt clearly understood that they would be killed if the town, or state, or tribe by which they were given should misbehave, or in any way thwart the great conqueror.

The Ambiani come next, and the ancestors of our intimate friends at Amiens soon give themselves up. The next to them are the Nervii, a people far away to the north, where Lille now is and a considerable portion of Flanders. Of these Cæsar had heard wonderful travellers' tales. They were a people who admitted no dealers among them, being in this respect very unlike their descendants, the Belgians of to-day; they drank no wine, and indulged in no luxuries, lest their martial valour should be diminished. They send no ambassadors to Cæsar, and resolve to hold their own if they can. They trust solely to infantry in battle, and know nothing of horses. Against the cavalry of other nations, however, they are wont to protect themselves by artificial hedges, which they make almost as strong as walls.

Cæsar in attacking the Nervii had eight legions, and he tells us how he advanced against them "consuetudine suâ," — after his usual fashion. For some false information had been given to the Nervii on this subject, which brought them into considerable trouble. He sent on first his cavalry, then six legions, the legions consisting solely of foot-soldiers; after these all the baggage, commissariat, and burden of the army, comprising the materials necessary for sieges; and lastly, the two other legions, which had been latest enrolled. It may be as well to explain here that the legion in the time of Cæsar consisted on paper of six thousand heavy-armed foot-soldiers. There were ten cohorts in a legion, and six centuries, or six hundred men, in each cohort. It may possibly be that, as with our regiments, the numbers were frequently not full. Eight full legions would thus have formed an army consisting of 48,000 infantry. The exact number of men under his orders Cæsar does not mention here or elsewhere.

According to his own showing, Cæsar is hurried into a battle before he knows where he is. Cæsar, he says, had everything to do himself, all at the same time,—to unfurl the standard of battle, to give the signal with the trumpet, to get back the soldiers from their work, to call back some who had gone to a distance for stuff to make a rampart, to draw up the army, to address the men, and then to give the word. In that matter of oratory, he only tells them to remember their old valour. The enemy was so close upon them, and so ready for fighting, that they could scarcely put on their helmets and take their shields out of their cases. So great was the confusion that the soldiers could not get to their own ranks, but had to fight as they stood, under any flag that was nearest to them. There were so many things against them, and especially those thick artificial hedges, which prevented them even from seeing, that it was impossible for them to fight according to any method, and in consequence there were vicissitudes of fortune. One is driven to feel that on this occasion Cæsar was caught napping. The Nervii did at times and places seem to be getting the best of it. The ninth and tenth legions pursue one tribe into a river, and then they have to fight them again, and drive them out of the river. The eleventh and eighth, having put to flight another tribe, are attacked on the very river-banks. The twelfth and the seventh have their hands equally full, when Boduognatus, the Nervian chief, makes his way into the very middle of the Roman camp. So great is the confusion that the Treviri, who had joined Cæsar on this occasion as allies, although reputed the bravest of the cavalry of Gaul, run away home, and declare that the Romans are conquered. Cæsar, however, comes to the rescue, and saves his army on this occasion by personal prowess. When he saw how it was going,—"rem esse in angusto,"—how the thing had got itself into the very narrowest neck of a difficulty, he seizes a shield from a common soldier,—having come there himself with no shield,—and rushes into the fight. When the soldiers saw him, and saw, too, that what they did was done in his sight, they fought anew, and the onslaught of the enemy was checked.

Perhaps readers will wish that they could know how much of all this is exactly true. It reads as though it were true. We cannot in these days understand how one brave man at such a moment should be so much more effective than another, how he should be known personally to the soldiers of an army so large, how Cæsar should have known the names of the centurions,—for he tells us that he addresses them by name;—and yet it reads like truth; and the reader feels that as Cæsar would hardly condescend to boast, so neither would he be constrained by any modern feeling of humility from telling any truth of himself. It is as though Minerva were to tell us of some descent which she made among the Trojans. The Nervii fight on, but of course they are driven in flight. The nation is all but destroyed, so that the very name can but hardly remain;—so at least we are told here, though we hear of them again as a tribe by no means destroyed or powerless. When out of six hundred senators there are but three senators left, when from sixty thousand fighting men the army has been reduced to scarcely five hundred, Cæsar throws the mantle of his mercy over the survivors. He allows them even to go and live in their own homes, and forbids their neighbours to harass them. There can be no doubt that Cæsar nearly got the worst of it in this struggle, and we may surmise that he learned a lesson which was of service to him in subsequent campaigns.

But there are still certain Aduatici to be disposed of before the summer is over,—people who had helped the Nervii,—who have a city of their own, and who live somewhere in the present Namur district.[6] At first they fight a little round the walls of their town; but when they see what terrible instruments Cæsar has, by means of which to get at them over their very walls,—how he can build up a great turret at a distance, which, at that distance, is ludicrous to them, but which he brings near to them, so that it overhangs them, from which to harass them with arrows and stones, and against which, so high is it, they have no defence—then they send out and beg for mercy. Surely, they say, Cæsar and the Romans must have more than human power. They will give up everything, if only Cæsar out of his mercy will leave to them their arms. They are always at war with all their neighbours; and where would they be without arms?

Cæsar replies. Merits of their own they have none. How could a tribe have merits against which Cæsar was at war? Nevertheless, such being his custom, he will admit them to some terms of grace if they surrender before his battering-ram has touched their walls. But as for their arms, surely they must be joking with him. Of course their arms must be surrendered. What he had done for the Nervii he would do for them. He would tell their neighbours not to hurt them. They agree, and throw their arms into the outside ditch of the town, but not quite all their arms. A part,—a third,—are cunningly kept back; and when Cæsar enters the town, they who have kept their arms, and others unarmed, try to escape from the town. They fight, and some thousands are slain. Others are driven back, and these are sold for slaves. Who, we wonder, could have been the purchasers, and at what price on that day was a man to be bought in the city of the Aduatici?

Then Cæsar learns through his lieutenant, young Crassus, the son of his colleague in the triumvirate, that all the Belgian states, from the Scheldt to the Bay of Biscay, have been reduced beneath the yoke of the Roman people. The Germans, too, send ambassadors to him, so convinced are they that to fight against him is of no avail,—so wonderful an idea of this last war has pervaded all the tribes of barbarians. But Cæsar is in a hurry, and can hear no ambassadors now. He wants to get into Italy, and they must come again to him next summer.

For all which glorious doings a public thanksgiving of fifteen days is decreed, as soon as the news is heard in Rome.

---

[6] These people were the descendants of those Cimbri who, half a century before, had caused such woe to Rome! The Cimbri, we are told, had gone forth from their lands, and had been six times victorious over Roman armies, taking possession of "our Province," and threatening Italy and Rome. The whole empire of the Republic had been in danger, but was at last saved by the courage, skill, and rapidity of Marius. In going forth from their country they had left a remnant behind with such of their possessions as they could not carry with them; and these Aduatici were the children and grandchildren of that remnant. Cæsar doubtless remembered it all.

CHAPTER IV.

Third Book Of The War In Gaul.—Cæsar Subdues The Western Tribes Of Gaul.—B.C. 56.

In the first few lines of the third book we learn that Cæsar had an eye not only for conquest, but for the advantages of conquest also. When he went into Italy at the end of the last campaign, he sent one Galba, whose descendant became emperor after Nero, with the twelfth legion, to take up his winter quarters in the upper valley of the Rhone, in order that an easier traffic might be opened to traders passing over the Alps in and out of Northern Italy. It seems that the passage used was that of the Great St Bernard, and Galba placed himself with his legion at that junction of the valley which we all know so well as Martigny. Here, however, he was attacked furiously in his camp by the inhabitants of the valley, who probably objected to being dictated to as to the amount of toll to be charged upon the travelling traders, and was very nearly destroyed. The Romans, however, at last, when they had neither weapons nor food left for maintaining their camp, resolved to cut their way through their enemies. This they did so effectually that they slaughtered more than ten thousand men, and the other twenty thousand of Swiss warriors all took to flight! Nevertheless Galba thought it as well to leave that inhospitable region, in which it was almost impossible to find food for the winter, and took himself down the valley and along the lake to the Roman Province. He made his winter-quarters among the Allobroges, who belonged to the Province,—a people living just south of the present Lyons. How the Allobroges liked it we are not told, but we know that they were then very faithful, although in former days they had given great trouble. Their position made faith to Rome almost a necessity. Whether, in such a position, Cæsar's lieutenants paid their way, and bought their corn at market price, we do not know. It was Cæsar's rule, no doubt, to make the country on which his army stood support his army.

When the number of men whom Cæsar took with him into countries hitherto unknown to him or his army is considered, and the apparently reckless audacity with which he did so, it must be acknowledged that he himself says very little about his difficulties. He must constantly have had armies for which to provide twice as large as our Crimean army,—probably as large as the united force of the English and French in the Crimea; and he certainly could not bring with him what he wanted in ships. The road from Balaclava up to the heights over Sebastopol, we know, was very bad; but it was short. The road from the foot of the Alps in the Roman province to the countries with which we were dealing in the last chapter could not, we should say, have been very good two thousand years ago, and it certainly was very long;—nearly a hundred miles for Cæsar to every single one of those that were so terrible to us in the Crimea. Cæsar, however, carried but little with him beyond his arms and implements of war, and of those the heaviest he no doubt made as he went. The men had an allowance of corn per day, besides so much pay. We are told that the pay before Cæsar's time was 100 *asses* a-month for the legionaries,—the *as* being less than a penny,—and that this was doubled by Cæsar. We can conceive that the money troubled him comparatively slightly, but that the finding of the daily corn and forage for so large a host of men and horses must have been very difficult. He speaks of the difficulty often, but never with that despair which was felt as to the roasting of our coffee in the Crimea. We hear of his waiting till forage should have grown, and sometimes there are necessary considerations "de re frumentariâ,"—about that great general question of provisions; but of crushing difficulties very little is said, and of bad roads not a word. One great advantage Cæsar certainly had over Lord Raglan;—he was his own special correspondent. Coffee his men certainly did not get; but if their corn were not properly roasted for them, and if, as would be natural, the men grumbled, he had with him no licensed collector of grumbles to make public the sufferings of his men.

And now, when this affair of Galba's had been finished,—when Cæsar, as he tells us, really did think that all Gaul was "pacatam," tranquillised, or at least subdued,—the Belgians conquered, the Germans driven off, those Swiss fellows cut to pieces in the valley of the Rhone; when he thought that he might make a short visit into that other province of his, Illyricum, so that he might see what that was like,—he is told that another war has sprung up in Gaul! Young Crassus, with that necessity which of course was on him of providing winter food for the seventh legion which he had been ordered to take into Aquitania, has been obliged to send out for corn into the neighbouring countries. Of course a well-instructed young general, such as was Crassus, had taken hostages before he sent his men out among strange and wild barbarians. But in spite of that, the Veneti, a maritime people of ancient Brittany, just in that country of the Morbihan whither we now go to visit the works of the Druids at Carnac and Locmariaker, absolutely detained his two ambassadors;—so called afterwards, though in his first mention of them Cæsar names them as præfects and tribunes of the soldiers. Vannes, the capital of the department of the Morbihan, gives us a trace of the name of this tribe. The Veneti, who were powerful in ships, did not see why they should give their corn to Crassus. Cæsar, when he hears that ambassadors,—sacred ambassadors,—have been stopped, is filled with shame and indignation, and hurries off himself to look after the affair, having, as we may imagine, been able to see very little of Illyricum.

This horror of Cæsar in regard to his ambassadors,—in speaking of which he alludes to what the Gauls themselves felt when they came to understand what a thing they had done in making ambassadors prisoners,—"legatos,"—a name that has always been held sacred and inviolate among all nations,—is very great, and makes him feel that he must really be in earnest. We are reminded of the injunctions, printed in Spanish, which the Spaniards distributed among the Indians of the continent, in the countries now called Venezuela and New Granada, explaining to the people, who knew nothing of Spanish or of printing, how they were bound to obey the orders of a distant king, who had the authority of a more distant Pope, who again,—so they claimed,—was delegated by a more distant God. The pain of history consists in the injustice of the wolf towards the lamb, joined to the conviction that thus, and no otherwise, could the lamb be brought to better than a sheepish mode of existence! But Cæsar was in earnest.[7] The following is a translation of the tenth section of this book; "There were these difficulties in carrying on the war which we have above shown."—He alludes to the maritime capacities of the people whom he desires to conquer.—"Many things, nevertheless, urged Cæsar on to this war;—the wrongs of those Roman knights who had been detained, rebellion set on foot after an agreed surrender,"—that any such surrender had been made we do not hear, though we do hear, incidentally, that Crassus had taken hostages;—"a falling off from alliance after hostages had been given; conspiracy among so many tribes; and then this first consideration, that if this side of the country were disregarded, the other tribes might learn to think that they might take the same liberty. Then, when he bethought himself that, as the Gauls were prone to rebellion, and were quickly and easily excited to war, and that all men, moreover, are fond of liberty and hate a condition of subjection, he resolved that it would be well, rather than that other states should conspire,"—and to avoid the outbreak on behalf of freedom which might thus probably be made,—"that his army should be divided, and scattered about more widely." Treating all Gaul as a chess-board, he sends round to provide that the Treviri should be kept quiet. Headers will remember how far Treves is distant from the extremities of Brittany. The Belgians are to be looked to, lest they should rise and come and help. The Germans are to be prevented from crossing the Rhine. Labienus, who, during the Gallic wars, was Cæsar's general highest in trust, is to see to all this. Crassus is to go back into Aquitania and keep the south quiet. Titurius Sabinus, destined afterwards to a sad end, is sent with three legions,—eighteen thousand men,—among the neighbouring tribes of Northern Brittany and Normandy. "Young" Decimus Brutus,—Cæsar speaks of him with that kind affection which the epithet conveys, and we remember, as we read, that this Brutus appears afterwards in history as one of Cæsar's slayers, in conjunction with his greater namesake,—young Decimus Brutus, the future conspirator in Rome, has confided to him the fleet which is to destroy these much less guilty distant conspirators, and Cæsar himself takes the command of his own legions on the spot. All this is told in fewer words than are here used in describing the telling, and the reader feels that he has to do with a mighty man, whose eyes are everywhere, and of whom an ordinary enemy would certainly say, Surely this is no man, but a god.

He tells us how great was the effect of his own presence on the shore, though the battle was carried on under young Brutus at sea. "What remained of the conflict," he says, after describing their manœuvres, "depended on valour, in which

---

[7] And Cæsar was no doubt indignant as well as earnest, though, perhaps, irrational in his indignation. We know how sacred was held to be the person of the Roman citizen, and remember Cicero's patriotic declaration, "Facinus est vinciri civem Romanum,—scelus verberari;" and again, the words which Horace puts into the mouth of Regulus when he asserts that the Roman soldier must be lost for ever in his shame, and useless, "Qui lora restrictis lacertis Sensit iners timuitque mortem."

our men were far away the superior; and this was more especially true because the affair was carried on so plainly in the sight of Cæsar and the whole army that no brave deed could pass unobserved. For all the hills and upper lands, from whence the view down upon the sea was close, were covered by the army."

Of course he conquers the Veneti and other sea-going tribes, even on their own element. Whereupon they give themselves and all their belongings up to Cæsar. Cæsar, desirous that the rights of ambassadors shall hereafter be better respected among barbarians, determines that he must use a little severity. "Gravius vindicandum statuit;" — "he resolved that the offence should be expiated with more than ordinary punishment." Consequently, he kills all the senate, and sells all the other men as slaves! The pithy brevity, the unapologetic dignity of the sentence, as he pronounced it and tells it to us, is heartrending, but, at this distance of time, delightful also. "Itaque, omni senatu necato, reliquos sub coronâ vendidit;" — "therefore, all the senate having been slaughtered, he sold the other citizens with chaplets on their heads;" — it being the Roman custom so to mark captives in war intended for sale. We can see him as he waves his hand and passes on. Surely he must be a god!

His generals in this campaign are equally successful. One Viridovix, a Gaul up in the Normandy country, — somewhere about Avranches or St Lo, we may imagine, — is entrapped into a fight, and destroyed with his army. Aquitania surrenders herself to Crassus, after much fighting, and gives up her arms.

Then Cæsar reflects that the Morini and the Menapii had as yet never bowed their heads to him. Boulogne and Calais stand in the now well-known territory of the Morini, but the Menapii lie a long way off, up among the mouths of the Scheldt and the Rhine, — the Low Countries of modern history, — an uncomfortable people then, who would rush into their woods and marshes after a spell of fighting, and who seemed to have no particular homes or cities that could be attacked or destroyed. It was nearly the end of summer just now, and the distance between, let us say, Vannes in Brittany, and Breda, or even Antwerp, seems to us to be considerable, when we remember the condition of the country, and the size of Cæsar's army. But he had a few weeks to fill up, and then he might feel that all Gaul had been "pacified." At present there was this haughty little northern corner. "Omni Galliâ pacatâ, Morini Menapiique supererant;" — "all Gaul having been pacified, the Morini and Menapii remained." He was, moreover, no doubt beginning to reflect that from the Morini could be made the shortest journey into that wild Ultima Thule of an island in which lived the Britanni. Cæsar takes advantage of the few weeks, and attacks these uncomfortable people. When they retreat into the woods, he cuts the woods down. He does cut down an immense quantity of wood, but the enemy only recede into thicker and bigger woods. Bad weather comes on, and the soldiers can no longer endure life in their skin tents. Let us fancy these Italians encountering winter in undrained Flanders, with no walls or roofs to protect them, and ordered to cut down interminable woods! Had a 'Times' been then written and filed, instead of a "Commentary" from the hands of the General-in-chief, we should probably have heard of a good deal of suffering. As it is, we are only told that Cæsar had to give up his enterprise for that year. He therefore burned all their villages, laid waste all their fields, and then took his army down into a more comfortable region south of the Seine, and there put them into winter quarters,—not much to the comfort of the people there residing.

CHAPTER V.

Fourth Book Of The War In Gaul. — Cæsar Crosses The Rhine, Slaughters The Germans, And Goes Into Britain. — B.C. 55.

In the next year certain Germans, Usipetes and others, crossed the Rhine into Gaul, not far from the sea, as Cæsar tells us. He tells us again, that when he drove the Germans back over the river, it was near the confluence of the Meuse and the Rhine. When we remember how difficult it was for Cæsar to obtain information, we must acknowledge that his geography as to the passage of the Rhine out to the sea, and of the junction of the Rhine and the Meuse by the Waal, is wonderfully correct. The spot indicated as that at which the Germans were driven into the river would seem to be near Bommel in Holland, where the Waal and the Meuse join their waters, at the head of the island of Bommel, where Fort St André stands, or stood.[8]

Those wonderful Suevi, among whom the men alternately fight and plough, year and year about, caring more, however, for cattle than they do for corn, who are socialists in regard to land, having no private property in their fields, — who, all of them, from their youth upwards, do just what they please, — large, bony men, who wear, even in these cold regions, each simply some scanty morsel of skin covering, — who bathe in rivers all the year through, who deal with traders only to sell the spoils of war, who care but little for their horses, and ride, when they do ride, without saddles, — thinking nothing of men to whom such delicate appendages are necessary, — who drink no wine, and will have no neighbours near them, — these ferocious Suevi have driven other German tribes over the Rhine into Gaul. Cæsar, hearing this, is filled with apprehension. He knows the weakness of his poor friends the Gauls, — how prone they are to gossiping, of what a restless temper. It is in the country of the Menapii, the tribe with which he did not quite finish his little affair in the last chapter, that these Germans are settling; and there is no knowing what trouble the intruders may give him if he allows them to make themselves at home on that side of the river. So he hurries off to give help to the

---

[8] Cæsar speaks of the confluence of the Rhine and the "Mosa" as the spot at which he drove the Germans into the river, — and in various passages, speaking of the Mosa, clearly means the Meuse. It appears, however, to be the opinion of English scholars who have studied the topography of Cæsar's campaigns with much labour, that the confluence of the Moselle and Rhine, from which Coblentz derives its name, is the spot intended. Napoleon, who has hardly made himself an authority on the affairs of Cæsar generally, but who is thought to be an authority in regard to topography, holds to the opinion that the site in Holland is intended to be described. Readers who are anxious on the subject can choose between the two; but readers who are not anxious will probably be more numerous.

poor Menapii.

Of course there is a sending of ambassadors. The Germans acknowledge that they have been turned out of their own lands by their brethren, the Suevi, who are better men than they are. But they profess that, in fighting, the Suevi, and the Suevi only, are their masters. Not even the immortal gods can stand against the Suevi. But they also are Germans, and are not at all afraid of the Romans. But in the proposition which they make they show some little awe. Will Cæsar allow them to remain where they are, or allot to them some other region on that side of the Rhine? Cæsar tells them that they may go and live, if they please, with the Ubii, — another tribe of Germans who occupy the Rhine country, probably where Cologne now stands, or perhaps a little north of it, and who seem already to have been forced over the Rhine, — they, or some of them, — and to have made good their footing somewhere in the region in which Charlemagne built his church, now called Aix-la-Chapelle. There they are, Germans still, and probably are so because these Ubii made good their footing. The Ubii also are in trouble with the Suevi; and if these intruders will go and join the Ubii, Cæsar will make it all straight for them. The intruders hesitate, but do not go, and at last attack Cæsar's cavalry, not without some success. During this fight there is double treachery, — first on the part of the Germans, and then on Cæsar's part, — which is chiefly memorable for the attack made on Cæsar in Rome. It was in consequence of the deceit here practised that it was proposed by his enemies in the city that he should be given up by the Republic to the foe. Had any such decree been passed, it would not have been easy to give up Cæsar.

The Germans are, of course, beaten, and they are driven into the river on those low and then undrained regions in which the Rhine and the Meuse and the Waal confuse themselves and confuse travellers; — either here, or much higher up the river at Coblentz; but the reader will already have settled that question for himself at the beginning of the chapter. Cæsar speaks of these Germans as though they were all drowned, — men, women, and children. They had brought their entire families with them, and, when the fighting went against them, with their entire families they fled into the river. Cæsar was pursuing them after the battle, and they precipitated themselves over the banks. There, overcome by fear, fatigue, and the waters, they perished. There was computed to be a hundred and eighty thousand of them who were destroyed; but the Roman army was safe to a man.[9]

Then Cæsar made up his mind to cross the river. It seems that he had no intention of extending the empire of the Republic into what he called Germany, but that he thought it necessary to frighten the Germans. The cavalry of those intruding Usipetes had, luckily for them, been absent, foraging over the river; and he now sent to the Sigambri, among whom they had taken refuge, desiring that these horsemen should be given up to him. But the Sigambri will not obey. The Germans seem to have understood that Cæsar had Gaul in his hands, to do as he liked with it; but they grudged his interference beyond the Rhine. Cæsar, however, always managed to have a set of friends among his enemies, to help him in adjusting his

---

[9] "Hostium numerus capitum CDXXX millium fuisset," from which words we are led to suppose that there were 180,000 fighting men, besides the women and children.

enmities. We have heard of the Ædui in central Gaul, and of the Remi in the north. The Ubii were his German friends, who were probably at this time occupying both banks of the river; and the Ubii ask him just to come over and frighten their neighbours. Cæsar resolves upon gratifying them. And as it is not consistent either with his safety or with his dignity to cross the river in boats, he determines to build a bridge.

Is there a schoolboy in England, or one who has been a schoolboy, at any Cæsar-reading school, who does not remember those memorable words, "Tigna bina sesquipedalia," with which Cæsar begins his graphic account of the building of the bridge? When the breadth of the river is considered, its rapidity, and the difficulty which there must have been in finding tools and materials for such a construction, in a country so wild and so remote from Roman civilisation, the creation of this bridge fills us with admiration for Cæsar's spirit and capacity. He drove down piles into the bed of the river, two and two, prone against the stream. We could do that now, though hardly as quickly as Cæsar did it; but we should want coffer-dams and steam-pumps, patent rammers, and a clerk of the works. He explains to us that he so built the foundations that the very strength of the stream added to their strength and consistency. In ten days the whole thing was done, and the army carried over. Cæsar does not tell us at what suffering, or with the loss of how many men. It is the simplicity of everything which is so wonderful in these Commentaries. We have read of works constructed by modern armies, and of works which modern armies could not construct. We remember the road up from Balaclava, and the railway which was sent out from England. We know, too, what are the aids and appliances with which science has furnished us. But yet in no modern warfare do the difficulties seem to have been so light, so little worthy of mention, as they were to Cæsar. He made his bridge and took over his army, cavalry and all, in ten days. There must have been difficulty and hardship, and the drowning, we should fear, of many men; but Cæsar says nothing of all this.

Ambassadors immediately are sent. From the moment in which the bridge was begun, the Sigambri ran away and hid themselves in the woods. Cæsar burns all their villages, cuts down all their corn, and travels down into the country of the Ubii. He comforts them; and tidings of his approach then reach those terrible Suevi. They make ready for war on a grand scale; but Cæsar, reflecting that he had not brought his army over the river for the sake of fighting the Suevi, and telling us that he had already done enough for honour and for the good of the cause, took his army back after eighteen days spent in the journey, and destroyed his bridge.

Then comes a passage which makes a Briton vacillate between shame at his own ancient insignificance, and anger at Cæsar's misapprehension of his ancient character. There were left of the fighting season after Cæsar came back across the Rhine just a few weeks; and what can he do better with them than go over and conquer Britannia? This first record of an invasion upon us comes in at the fag-end of a chapter, and the invasion was made simply to fill up the summer! Nobody, Cæsar tells us, seemed to know anything about the island; and yet it was the fact that in all his wars with the Gauls, the Gauls were helped by men out of Britain. Before he will face the danger with his army he sends over a trusty messenger, to look about and find out something as to the coasts and harbours. The trusty messenger does not dare to disembark, but comes back and tells Cæsar what he has seen from his ship. Cæsar, in the mean time, has got together a great fleet somewhere in the Boulogne and Calais country; and,—so he says,—messengers have come to him from Britain, whither rumours of his purpose have already flown, saying that they will submit themselves to the Roman Republic. We may believe just as much of that as we please. But he clearly thinks less of the Boulogne and Calais people than he does even of the Britons, which is a comfort to us. When these people,—then called Morini,—came to him, asking pardon for having dared to oppose him once before, and offering any number of hostages, and saying that they had been led on by bad advice, Cæsar admitted them into some degree of grace; not wishing, as he tells us, to be kept out of Britain by the consideration of such very small affairs. "Neque has tantularum rerum occupationes sibi Britanniæ anteponendas judicabat." We hope that the Boulogne and Calais people understand and appreciate the phrase. Having taken plenty of hostages, he determines to trust the Boulogne and Calais people, and prepares his ships for passing the Channel. He starts nearly at the third watch,—about midnight, we may presume. A portion of his army,—the cavalry,—encounter some little delay, such as has often occurred on the same spot since, even to travellers without horses. He himself got over to the British coast at about the fourth hour. This, at midsummer, would have been about a quarter past eight. As it was now late in the summer, it may have been nine o'clock in the morning when Cæsar found himself under the cliffs of Kent, and saw our armed ancestors standing along all the hills ready to meet him. He stayed at anchor, waiting for his ships, till about two P.M. His cavalry did not get across till four days afterwards. Having given his orders, and found a fitting moment and a fitting spot, Cæsar runs his ships up upon the beach.

Cæsar confesses to a good deal of difficulty in getting ashore. When we know how very hard it is to accomplish the same feat, on the same coast, in these days, with all the appliances of modern science to aid us, and, as we must presume, with no real intention on the part of the Cantii, or men of Kent, to oppose our landing, we can quite sympathise with Cæsar. The ships were so big that they could not be brought into very shallow water. The Roman soldiers were compelled to jump into the sea, heavily armed, and there to fight with the waves and with the enemy. But the Britons, having the use of all their limbs, knowing the ground, standing either on the shore or just running into the shallows, made the landing uneasy enough. "Nostri,"—our men,—says Cæsar, with all these things against them, were not all of them so alert at fighting as was usual with them on dry ground;—at which no one can be surprised.

Cæsar had two kinds of ships—"naves longæ," long ships for carrying soldiers; and "naves onerariæ," ships for carrying burdens. The long ships do not seem to have been such ships of war as the Romans generally used in their seafights, but were handier, and more easily worked, than the transports. These he laid broadside to the shore, and harassed the poor natives with stones and arrows. Then the eagle-bearer of the tenth legion jumped into the sea, proclaiming that he, at any rate, would do his duty. Unless they wished to see their eagle fall into the hands of the enemy, they must follow him. "Jump down, he said, my fellow-soldiers, unless you wish to betray your eagle to the enemy. I at least will do my duty to the Republic and to our General. When he had said this with a loud voice, he threw himself out of the ship and advanced the eagle against the enemy." Seeing and hearing this, the men leaped forth freely, from that ship and from others. As usual, there was some sharp fighting. "Pugnatum est ab utrisque acriter." It is nearly always the same thing. Cæsar throws away none of his glory by underrating his enemy. But at length the Britons fly. "This thing only was wanting to Cæsar's usual good fortune,"—that he was deficient in cavalry wherewith to ride on in pursuit, and "take the island!" Considering how very short a time he remains in the island, we feel that his complaint against fortune is hardly well founded. But there is a general surrender, and a claiming of hostages, and after a few days a sparkle of new hope in the breasts of the Britons. A storm arises, and Cæsar's ships are so knocked about that he does not know how he will get back to Gaul. He is troubled by a very high tide, not understanding the nature of these tides. As he had only intended this for a little tentative trip,—a mere taste of a future war with Britain,—he had brought no large supply of corn with him. He must get back, by hook or by crook. The Britons, seeing how it is with him, think that they can destroy him, and make an attempt to do so. The seventh legion is in great peril, having been sent out to find corn, but is rescued. Certain of his ships,—those which had been most grievously handled by the storm,—he breaks up, in order that he may mend the others with their materials. When we think how long it takes us to mend ships, having dockyards, and patent slips, and all things ready, this is most marvellous to us. But he does mend his ships, and while so doing he has a second fight with the Britons, and again repulses them. There is a burning and destroying of everything far and wide, a gathering of ambassadors to Cæsar asking for terms, a demand for hostages,—a double number of hostages now,—whom Cæsar desired to have sent over to him to Gaul, because at this time of the year he did not choose to trust them to ships that were unseaworthy; and he himself, with all his army, gets back into the Boulogne and Calais country. Two transports only are missing, which are carried somewhat lower down the coast. There are but three hundred men in these transports, and these the Morini of those parts threaten to kill unless they will give up their arms. But Cæsar sends help, and even these three hundred are saved from disgrace. There is, of course, more burning of houses and laying waste of fields because of this little attempt, and then Cæsar puts his army into winter quarters.

What would have been the difference to the world if the Britons, as they surely might have done, had destroyed Cæsar and every Roman, and not left even a ship to get back to Gaul? In lieu of this Cæsar could send news to Rome of these various victories, and have a public thanksgiving decreed,—on this occasion for twenty days.

CHAPTER VI.

Fifth Book Of The War In Gaul.—Cæsar's Second Invasion Of Britain.—The Gauls Rise Against Him.—B.C. 54.

On his return out of Britain, Cæsar, as usual, went over the Alps to look after his other provinces, and to attend to his business in Italy; but he was determined to make another raid upon the island. He could not yet assume that he had "taken it," and therefore he left minute instructions with his generals as to the building of more ships, and the repair of those which had been so nearly destroyed. He sends to Spain, he tells us, for the things necessary to equip his ships. We never hear of any difficulty about money. We know that he did obtain large grants from Rome for the support of his legions; but no scruple was made in making war maintain war, as far as such maintenance could be obtained. Cæsar personally was in an extremity of debt when he commenced his campaigns. He had borrowed an enormous sum, eight hundred and thirty talents, or something over £200,000, from Crassus,—who was specially the rich Roman of those days,—before he could take charge of his Spanish province. When his wars were over, he returned to Rome with a great treasure; and indeed during these wars in Gaul he expended large sums in bribing Romans. We may suppose that he found hoards among the barbarians, as Lord Clive did in the East Indies. Clive contented himself with taking some: Cæsar probably took all.

Having given the order about his ships, he settled a little matter in Illyricum, taking care to raise some tribute there also. He allows but a dozen lines for recording this winter work, and then tells us that he hurried back to his army and his ships. His command had been so well obeyed in regard to vessels, that he finds ready, of that special sort which he had ordered with one bank of oars only on each side, as many as six hundred, and twenty-eight of the larger sort. He gives his soldiers very great credit for their exertions, and sends his fleet to the Portus Itius. The exact spot which Cæsar called by this name the geographers have not identified, but it is supposed to be between Boulogne and Calais. It may probably have been at Wissant. Having seen that things were thus ready for a second trip into Britain, he turns round and hurries off with four legions and eight hundred cavalry,—an army of 25,000 men,—into the Treves country. There is a quarrel going on there between two chieftains which it is well that he should settle,—somewhat as the monkey settled the contest about the oyster. This, however, is a mere nothing of an affair, and he is back again among his ships at the Portus Itius in a page and a half.

He resolves upon taking five legions of his own soldiers into Britain, and two thousand mounted Gauls. He had brought together four thousand of these horsemen, collected from all Gaul, their chiefs and nobles, not only as fighting allies, but as hostages that the tribes should not rise in rebellion while his back was turned. These he divides, taking half with him, and leaving half with three legions of his own men, under Labienus, in the Boulogne country, as a base to his army, to look after the provisions, and to see that he be not harassed on his return. There is a little affair, however, with one of the Gaulish chieftains, Dumnorix the Æduan, who ought to have been his fastest friend. Dumnorix runs away with all the Æduan horsemen. Cæsar, however, sends after him and has him killed, and then all things are ready. He starts with altogether more than 800 ships at sunset, and comes over with a gentle south-west wind. He arrives off the coast of Britain at about noon, but can see none of the inhabitants on the cliff. He imagines that they have all fled, frightened by the number of his ships. Cæsar establishes his camp, and proceeds that same night about twelve miles into the country,—eleven miles, we may say, as our mile is longer than the Roman,—and there he finds the Britons. There is some fighting, after which Cæsar returns and fortifies his camp. Then there comes a storm and knocks his ships about terribly,—although he had found, as he thought, a nice soft place for them. But the tempest is very violent, and they are torn away from their anchors, and thrust upon the shore, and dashed against each other till there is infinite trouble. He is obliged to send over to Labienus, telling him to build more ships; and those which are left he drags up over the shore to his camp, in spite of the enormous labour required in doing it. He is ten days at this work, night and day, and we may imagine that his soldiers had not an easy time of it. When this has been done, he advances again into the country after the enemy, and finds that Cassivellaunus is in command of the united forces of the different tribes. Cassivellaunus comes from the other side of the Thames, over in Middlesex or Hertfordshire. The Britons had not hitherto lived very peaceably together, but now they agree that against the Romans they will act in union under Cassivellaunus.

Cæsar's description of the island is very interesting. The interior is inhabited by natives,—or rather by "aborigines." Cæsar states this at least as the tradition of the country. But the maritime parts are held by Belgian immigrants, who, for the most part, have brought with them from the Continent the names of their tribes. The population is great, and the houses, built very like the houses in Gaul, are numerous and very thick together. The Britons have a great deal of cattle. They use money, having either copper coin or iron rings of a great weight. Tin is found in the middle of the island, and, about the coast, iron. But the quantity of iron found is small. Brass they import. They have the same timber as in Gaul,—only they have neither beech nor fir. Hares and chickens and geese they think it wrong to eat; but they keep these animals as pets. The climate, on the whole, is milder than in Gaul. The island is triangular. One corner, that of Kent, has an eastern and a southern aspect. This southern side of the island he makes 500 miles, exceeding the truth by about 150 miles. Then Cæsar becomes a little hazy in his geography,—telling us that the other side, meaning the western line of the triangle, where Ireland lies, verges towards Spain. Ireland, he says, is half the size of Britain, and about the same distance from it that Britain is from Gaul. In the middle of the channel dividing Ireland from Britain there is an island called Mona,—the Isle of Man. There are also some other islands which at midwinter have thirty continuous days of night. Here Cæsar becomes not only hazy but mythic. But he explains that he has seen nothing of this himself, although he has ascertained, by scientific measurement, that the nights in Britain are shorter than on the Continent. Of course the nights are shorter with us in summer than they are in Italy, and longer in winter. The western coast he makes out to be 700 miles long; in saying which he is nearly 100 miles over the mark. The third side he describes as looking towards the north. He means the eastern coast. This he calls 800 miles long, and exaggerates our territories by more than 200 miles. The marvel, however, is that he should be so near the truth. The men of Kent are the most civilised: indeed they are almost as good as Gauls in this respect! What changes does not time make in the comparative merits of countries! The men in the interior live on flesh and milk, and do not care for corn. They wear skin clothing. They make themselves horrible with woad, and go about with very long hair. They shave close, except the head and upper lip. Then comes the worst habit of all;—ten or a dozen men have their wives in common between them.

We have a very vivid and by no means unflattering account of the singular agility of our ancestors in their mode of fighting from their chariots. "This," says Cæsar, "is the nature of their chariot-fighting. They first drive rapidly about the battle-field,—"per omnes partes,"—and throw their darts, and frequently disorder the ranks by the very terror occasioned by the horses and by the noise of the wheels; and when they have made their way through the bodies of the cavalry, they jump down and fight on foot. Then the charioteers go a little out of the battle, and so place their chariots that they may have a ready mode of returning should their friends be pressed by the number of their enemies. Thus they unite the rapidity of cavalry and the stability of infantry; and so effective do they become by daily use and practice, that they are accustomed to keep their horses, excited as they are, on their legs on steep and precipitous ground, and to manage and turn them very quickly, and to run along the pole and stand upon the yoke,"—by which the horses were held together at the collars,—"and again with the greatest rapidity to return to the chariot."[10] All which is very wonderful.

Of course there is a great deal of fighting, and the Britons soon learn by experience to avoid general engagements and maintain guerilla actions. Cæsar by degrees makes his way to the Thames, and with great difficulty gets his army over it. He can only do this at one place, and that badly. The site of this ford he does not describe to us. It is supposed to have been near the place which we now know as Sunbury. He does tell us that his men were so deep in the water that their

---

[10] All well-instructed modern Britons have learned from the old authorities that the Briton war-chariots were furnished with scythes attached to the axles,—from Pomponius Mela, the Roman geographer, and from Mrs Markham, among others. And Eugene Sue, in his novel translated into English under the name of the 'Rival Races,' explains how the Bretons on the other side of the water, in the Morbihan, used these scythes; and how, before a battle with Cæsar's legions, the wives of the warriors arranged the straps so that the scythes might be worked from the chariot like oars from a boat. But Cæsar says nothing of such scythes, and surely he would have done so had he seen them. The reader must choose between Cæsar's silence and the authority of Pomponius Mela, Mrs Markham, and Eugene Sue.

heads only were above the stream. But even thus they were so impetuous in their onslaught, that the Britons would not wait for them on the opposite bank, but ran away. Soon there come unconditional surrender, and hostages, and promises of tribute. Cassivellaunus, who is himself but a usurper, and therefore has many enemies at home, endeavours to make himself secure in a strong place or town, which is supposed to have been on or near the site of our St Albans. Cæsar, however, explains that the poor Britons give the name of a town,—"oppidum,"—to a spot in which they have merely surrounded some thick woods with a ditch and rampart. Cæsar, of course, drives them out of their woodland fortress, and then there quickly follows another surrender, more hostages, and the demand for tribute. Cæsar leaves his orders behind him, as though to speak were to be obeyed. One Mandubratius, and not Cassivellaunus, is to be the future king in Middlesex and Hertfordshire,—that is, over the Trinobantes who live there. He fixes the amount of tribute to be sent annually by the Britons to Rome; and he especially leaves orders that Cassivellaunus shall do no mischief to the young Mandubratius. Then he crosses back into Gaul at two trips,—his ships taking half the army first and coming back for the other half; and he piously observes that though he had lost many ships when they were comparatively empty, hardly one had been destroyed while his soldiers were in them.

So was ended Cæsar's second and last invasion of Britain. That he had reduced Britain as he had reduced Gaul he certainly could not boast;—though Quintus Cicero had written to his brother to say that Britannia was,—"confecta,"—finished. Though he had twice landed his army under the white cliffs, and twice taken it away with comparative security, he had on both occasions been made to feel how terribly strong an ally to the Britons was that channel which divided them from the Continent. The reader is made to feel that on both occasions the existence of his army and of himself is in the greatest peril. Cæsar's idea in attacking Britain was probably rather that of making the Gauls believe that his power could reach even beyond them,—could extend itself all round them, even into distant islands,— than of absolutely establishing the Roman dominion beyond that distant sea. The Britons had helped the Gauls in their wars with him, and it was necessary that he should punish any who presumed to give such help. Whether the orders which he left behind him were obeyed we do not know; but we may imagine that the tribute exacted was not sent to Rome with great punctuality. In fact, Cæsar invaded the island twice, but did not reduce it.

On his return to Gaul, nearly at the close of the summer, he found himself obliged to distribute his army about the country because of a great scarcity of provisions. There had been a drought, and the crops had failed. Hitherto he had kept his army together during the winter; now he was obliged to divide his legions, placing one with one tribe, and another with another. A legion and a half he stations under two of his generals, L. Titurius Sabinus, and L. Aurunculeius Cotta, among the Eburones, who live on the banks of the Meuse in the Liege and Namur country,—a very stout people, who are still much averse to the dominion of Rome. In this way he thought he might best get over that difficulty as to the scarcity of provisions; but yet he so well understood the danger of separating his army, that he is careful to tell us that, with the exception of one legion which he had stationed in a very quiet country,—among the Essui, where Alençon now stands,—they were all within a hundred miles of each other. Nevertheless, in spite of this precaution, there now fell upon Cæsar the greatest calamity which he had ever yet suffered in war.

During all these campaigns, the desire of the Gauls to free themselves from the power and the tyranny of Rome never ceased; nor did their intention to do so ever fade away. Cæsar must have been to them as a venomous blight, or some evil divinity sent to afflict them for causes which they could not understand. There were tribes who truckled to him, but he had no real friends among them. If any Gauls could have loved him, the Ædui should have done so; but that Dumnorix, the Æduan, who ran away with the horsemen of his tribe when he was wanted to help in the invasion of Britain, had, before he was killed, tried to defend himself, asserting vociferously that he was a free man and belonging to a free state. He had failed to understand that, in being admitted to the alliance of Cæsar, he was bound to obey Cæsar. Cæsar speaks of it all with his godlike simplicity, as though he saw nothing ungodlike in the work he was doing. There was no touch of remorse in him, as he ordered men to be slaughtered and villages to be burned. He was able to look at those things as trifles,—as parts of a great whole. He felt no more than does the gentleman who sends the sheep out of his park to be slaughtered at the appointed time. When he seems to be most cruel, it is for the sake of example,— that some politic result may follow,—that Gauls may know, and Italians know also, that they must bow the knee to Cæsar. But the heart of the reader is made to bleed as he sees the unavailing struggles of the tribes. One does not specially love the Ædui; but Dumnorix protesting that he will not return, that he is a free man, of a free state, and then being killed, is a man to be loved. Among the Carn- utes, where Chartres now stands, Cæsar has set up a pet king, one Tasgetius; but when Cæsar is away in Britain, the Carnutes kill Tasgetius. They will have no pet of Cæsar's. And now the stout Eburones, who have two kings of their own over them, Ambiorix and Cativolcus, understanding that Cæsar's difficulty is their op- portunity, attack the Roman camp, with its legion and a half of men under Titurius and Cotta.

Ambiorix, the chieftain, is very crafty. He persuades the Roman generals to send ambassadors to him, and to these he tells his story. He himself, Ambiorix, loves Cæsar beyond all things. Has not Cæsar done him great kindnesses? He would not willingly lift a hand against Cæsar, but he cannot control his state. The facts, however, are thus; an enormous body of Germans has crossed the Rhine, and is hurrying on to destroy that Roman camp; and it certainly will be destroyed, so great is the number of the Germans. Thus says Ambiorix; and then suggests whether it would not be well that Titurius and Cotta with their nine or ten thou- sand men,—a mere handful of men against all these Germans who are already over the Rhine;—would it not be well that the Romans should go and join some of their brethren, either the legion that is among the Nervii to the east, under Quintus Cicero, the brother of the great orator—or that other legion which Labienus has, a little to the south, on the borders of the Remi and Treviri? And in regard to a good turn on his own part, so great is the love and veneration which he, Ambiorix, feels for Cæsar, that he is quite ready to see the Romans safe through the territories of the Eburones. He begs Titurius and Cotta to think of this, and to allow him to aid them in their escape while escape is possible. The two Roman generals do think of it. Titurius thinks that it will be well to take the advice of Ambiorix. Cotta, and with him many of the tribunes and centurions of the soldiers, think that they should not stir without Cæsar's orders;—think also that there is nothing baser or more foolish in warfare than to act on advice given by an enemy. Titurius, however, is clear for going, and Cotta, after much argument and some invective, gives way. Early on the next morning they all leave their camp, taking with them their baggage, and marching forth as though through a friendly country,—apparently with belief in the proffered friendship of Ambiorix. The Eburones had of course prepared an ambush, and the Roman army is attacked both behind and before, and is thrown into utter confusion.

The legion, or legion and a half, with its two commanders, is altogether destroyed. Titurius goes out from his ranks to meet Ambiorix, and pray for peace. He is told to throw away his arms, and submitting to the disgrace, casts them down. Then, while Ambiorix is making a long speech, the Roman general is surrounded and slaughtered. Cotta is killed fighting; as also are more than half the soldiers. The rest get back into the camp at night, and then, despairing of any safety, overwhelmed with disgrace, conscious that there is no place for hope, they destroy themselves. Only a few have escaped during the fighting to tell the tale in the camp of Labienus.

As a rule the reader's sympathies are with the Gauls; but we cannot help feeling a certain regret that a Roman legion should have thus been wiled on to destruction through the weakness of its general. If Titurius could have been made to suffer alone we should bear it better. When we are told how the gallant eagle-bearer, Petrosidius, throws his eagle into the rampart, and then dies fighting before the camp, we wish that Ambiorix had been less successful. Of this, however, we feel quite certain, that there will come a day, and that soon, in which Cæsar will exact punishment.

Having done so much, Ambiorix and the Eburones do not desist. Now, if ever, after so great a disgrace, and with legions still scattered, may Cæsar be worsted. Q. Cicero is with his legion among the Nervii, and thither Ambiorix goes. The Nervii are quite ready, and Cicero is attacked in his camp. And here, too, for a long while it goes very badly with the Romans;—so badly that Cicero is hardly able to hold his ramparts against the attacks made upon them by the barbarians. Red-hot balls of clay and hot arrows are thrown into the camp, and there is a fire. The messengers sent to Cæsar for help are slain on the road, and the Romans begin to think that there is hardly a chance for them of escape. Unless Cæsar be with them they are not safe. All their power, their prestige, their certainty of conquest, lies in Cæsar. Cicero behaves like a prudent and a valiant man; but unless he had at last succeeded in getting a Gaulish slave to take a letter concealed in a dart to Cæsar, the enemy would have destroyed him.

There is a little episode of two Roman centurions, Pulfius and Varenus, who were always quarrelling as to which was the better man of the two. Pulfius with much bravado rushes out among the enemy, and Varenus follows him. Pulfius gets into trouble, and Varenus rescues him. Then Varenus is in a difficulty, and Pulfius comes to his assistance. According to all chances of war, both should have been killed; but both get back safe into the camp;—and nobody knows from that day to this which was the better man. Cæsar, of course, hastens to the assistance of his lieutenant, having sent word of his coming by a letter fastened to another dart, which, however, hardly reaches Cicero in time to comfort him before he sees the fires by which the coming legions wasted the country along their line of march. Then there is more fighting. Cæsar conquers, and Q. Cicero is rescued from his very disagreeable position. Labienus has also been in difficulty, stationed, as we remember, on the borders of the Treviri. The Treviri were quite as eager to attack him as the Eburones and Nervii to destroy the legions left in their territories. But before the attack is made, the news of Cæsar's victory, travelling with wonderful speed, is heard of in those parts, and the Treviri think it best to leave Labienus alone.

But Cæsar has perceived that, although he has so often boasted that all Gaul was at last at peace, all Gaul is prepared to carry on the war against him. It is during this winter that he seems to realise a conviction that his presence in the country is not popular with the Gauls in general, and that he has still much to do before he can make them understand that they are not free men, belonging to free states. The opposition to him has become so general that he himself determines to remain in Gaul all the winter; and even after telling us of the destruction of Indutiomarus, the chief of the Treviri, by Labienus, he can only boast that—"Cæsar had, after that was done, Gaul a little quieter,"—a little more like a subject country bound hand and foot,—than it was before. During this year Cæsar's proconsular power over his provinces was extended for a second period of five years.

CHAPTER VII.

Sixth Book Of The War In Gaul.—Cæsar Pursues Ambiorix.—The Manners Of The Gauls And Of The Germans Are Contrasted.—B.C. 53.

Cæsar begins the next campaign before the winter is over, having, as we have seen, been forced to continue the last long after the winter had commenced. The Gauls were learning to unite themselves, and things were becoming very serious with him. One Roman army, with probably ten thousand men, had been absolutely destroyed, with its generals Titurius Sabinus and Aurunculeius Cotta. Another under Quintus Cicero would have suffered the same fate, but for Cæsar's happy intervention. A third under Labienus had been attacked. All Gaul had been under arms, or thinking of arms, in the autumn; and though Cæsar had been able to report at the end of the campaign that Gaul,—his Gaul, as he intended that it should be,—was a little quieter, nevertheless he understood well that he still had his work to do before he could enter upon possession. He had already been the master of eight legions in Gaul, containing 48,000 foot-soldiers, levied on the Italian side of the Alps. He had added to this a large body of Gaulish cavalry and light infantry, over and above his eight legions. He had now lost an entire legion and a half, besides the gaps which must have been made in Britain, and by the loss of those who had fallen when attacked under Cicero by the Nervii. But he would show the Gauls that when so treated he could begin again, not only with renewed but with increased force. He would astound them by his display of Roman power, "thinking that, for the future, it would greatly affect the opinion of Gaul that the power of Italy should be seen to be so great that, if any reverse in war were suffered, not only could the injury be cured in a short time, but that the loss could be repaired even by increased forces." He not only levies fresh troops, but borrows a legion which Pompey commands outside the walls of Rome. He tells us that Pompey yields his legion to the "Republic and to Friendship." The Triumvirate was still existing, and Cæsar's great colleague probably felt that he had no alternative. In this way Cæsar not only re-established the legion which had been annihilated, but completes the others, and takes the field with two new legions added to his army. He probably now had as many as eighty thousand men under his command.

He first makes a raid against our old friends the Nervii, who had nearly conquered Cicero before Christmas, and who were already conspiring again with certain German and neighbouring Belgian tribes. The reader will perhaps remember that in the second book this tribe was said to have been so utterly destroyed that hardly their name remained. That, no doubt, was Cæsar's belief after the great slaughter. There had been, however, enough of them left nearly to destroy Q. Cicero and his legion. Then Cæsar goes to Paris,—Lutetia Parisiorum, of which we now hear for the first time,—and, with the help of his friends the Ædui and the Remi, makes a peace with the centre tribes of Gaul, the Senones and Carnutes. Then he resolves upon attacking Ambiorix with all his heart and soul. Ambiorix had destroyed his legion and killed his two generals, and against Ambiorix he must put forth all his force. It is said that when Cæsar first heard of that misfortune he swore that he would not cut his hair or shave himself till he was avenged. But he feels that he must first dispose of those who would naturally be the allies of this much-to-be-persecuted enemy. The Menapii, with whom we may remember that he had never quite settled matters in his former war, and who live on the southern banks of the Meuse not far from the sea, have not even yet sent to him messengers to ask for peace. He burns their villages, takes their cattle, makes slaves of the men, and then binds them by hostages to have no friendship with Ambiorix. In the mean time Labienus utterly defeats the great north-eastern tribe, the Treviri, whom he cunningly allures into fighting just before they are joined by certain Germans who are coming to aid them. "Quem Deus vult perdere prius dementat." These unfortunate Gauls and Germans fall into every trap that is laid for them. The speech which Cæsar quotes as having been made by Labienus to his troops on this occasion is memorable. "Now," says Labienus, "you have your opportunity. You have got your enemy thoroughly at advantage. That valour which you have so often displayed before the 'Imperator,' Cæsar, display now under my command. Think that Cæsar is present, and that he beholds you." To have written thus of himself Cæsar must have thought of himself as of a god. He tells the story as though it were quite natural that Labienus and the soldiers should so regard him.

After this battle, in which the Treviri are of course slaughtered, Cæsar makes a second bridge over the Rhine, somewhat above the spot at which he had crossed before. He does this, he says, for two reasons,—first, because the Germans had sent assistance to the Nervii; and secondly, lest his great enemy Ambiorix should find shelter among the Suevi. Then he suggests that the opportunity is a good one for saying something to his readers of the different manners of Gaul and of Germany. Among the Gauls, in their tribes, their villages, and even in their families, there are ever two factions, so that one should always balance the other, and neither become superior. Cæsar so tells us at this particular point of his narrative, because he is anxious to go back and explain how it was that he had taken the part of the Ædui, and had first come into conflict with the Germans, driving Ariovistus back across the Rhine for their sake. In eastern Gaul two tribes had long balanced each other, each, of course, striving for mastery,—the Ædui and the Sequani. The Sequani had called in the aid of the Germans, and the Ædui had been very hardly treated. In their sufferings they had appealed to Rome, having had former relations of close amity with the Republic. Divitiacus, their chief magistrate,—the brother of Dumnorix who was afterwards killed by Cæsar's order for running away with the Æduan cavalry before the second invasion of Britain,—had lived for a while in Rome, and had enjoyed Roman friendships, that of Cicero among others. There was a good deal of doubt in Rome as to what should be done with these Ædui; but at last, as we know, Cæsar decided on taking their part; and we know also how he drove Ariovistus back into Germany, with the loss of his wives and daughters. Thus it came to pass, Cæsar tells us, that the Ædui were accounted first of all the Gauls in regard to friendship with Rome; while the Remi, who came to his assistance so readily when the Belgians were in arms against him, were allowed the second place.

Among the Gauls there are, he says, two classes of men held in honour,—the Druids and the knights; by which we understand that two professions or modes of life, and two only, were open to the nobility,—the priesthood and the army. All the common people, Cæsar says, are serfs, or little better. They do not hesitate, when oppressed by debt or taxation, or the fear of some powerful enemy, to give themselves into slavery, loving the protection so obtained. The Druids have the chief political authority, and can maintain it by the dreadful power of excommunication. The excommunicated wretch is an outlaw, beyond the pale of civil rights. Over the Druids is one great Druid, at whose death the place is filled by election among all the Druids, unless there be one so conspicuously first that no ceremony of election is needed. Their most sacred spot for worship is among the Carnutes, in the middle of the country. Their discipline and mysteries came to them from Britain, and when any very knotty point arises they go to Britain to make inquiry. The Druids don't fight, and pay no taxes. The ambition to be a Druid is very great; but then so is the difficulty. Twenty years of tuition is not uncommonly needed; for everything has to be learned by heart. Of their religious secrets nothing may be written. Their great doctrine is the transmigration of souls; so that men should believe that the soul never dies, and that death, therefore, or that partial death which we see, need not be feared. They are great also in astronomy, geography, natural history,—and general theology, of course.

The knights, or nobles, have no resource but to fight. Cæsar suggests that before the blessing of his advent they were driven to the disagreeable necessity of fighting yearly with each other. Of all people the Gauls, he says, are the most given to superstition; in so much so, that in all dangers and difficulties they have recourse to human sacrifices, in which the Druids are their ministers. They burn their victims to appease their deities, and, by preference, will burn thieves and murderers,—the gods loving best such polluted victims,—but, in default of such, will have recourse to an immolation of innocents. Then Cæsar tells us that among the gods they chiefly worship Mercury, whom they seem to have regarded as the cleverest of the gods; but they also worship Apollo, Mars, Jove, and Minerva, ascribing to them the attributes which are allowed them by other nations. How the worship of the Greek and Roman gods became mingled with the religion of the Druids we are not told, nor does Cæsar express surprise that it should have been so. Cæsar gives the Roman names of these gods, but he does not intend us to understand that they were so called by the Gauls, who had their own names for their deities. The trophies of war they devote to Mars, and in many states keep large stores of such consecrated spoils. It is not often that a Gaul will commit the sacrilege of appropriating to his own use anything thus made sacred; but the punishment of such offence, when it is committed, is death by torture. There is the greatest veneration from sons to their fathers. Until the son can bear arms he does not approach his father, or even stand in public in his presence. The husband's fortune is made to equal the wife's dowry, and then the property is common between them. This seems well enough, and the law would suit the views of British wives of the present day. But the next Gaulish custom is not so well worthy of example. Husbands have the power of life and death over their wives and children; and when any man of mark dies, if there be cause for suspicion, his wives are examined under torture, and if any evil practice be confessed, they are then tortured to death. We learn from this passage that polygamy was allowed among the Gauls. The Gauls have grand funerals. Things which have been dear to the departed are burned at these ceremonies. Animals were thus burned in Cæsar's time, but in former days slaves also, and dependants who had been specially loved. The best-governed states are very particular in not allowing rumours as to state affairs to be made matter of public discussion. Anything heard is to be told to the magistrate; but there is to be no discussion on public affairs except in the public council. So much we hear of the customs of the Gauls.

The Germans differ from the Gauls in many things. They know nothing of Druids, nor do they care for sacrifices. They worship only what they see and enjoy,—the sun, and fire, and the moon. They spend their time in hunting and war, and care little for agriculture. They live on milk, cheese, and flesh. They are communists as to the soil, and stay no longer than a year on the same land. These customs they follow lest they should learn to prefer agriculture to war; lest they should grow fond of broad possessions, so that the rich should oppress the poor; lest they should by too much comfort become afraid of cold and heat; lest the love of money should grow among them, and one man should seek to be higher than another. From all which it seems that the Germans were not without advanced ideas in political economy.

It is a great point with the Germans to have no near neighbours. For the sake of safety and independence, each tribe loves to have a wide margin. In war the chieftains have power of life and death. In time of peace there are no appointed magistrates, but the chiefs in the cantons declare justice and quell litigation as well as they can. Thieving in a neighbouring state,—not in his own,—is honourable to a German. Expeditions for thieving are formed, which men may join or not as they please; but woe betide him who, having promised, fails. They are good to travelling strangers. There was a time when the Gauls were better men than the Germans, and could come into Germany and take German land. Even now, says Cæsar, there are Gaulish tribes living in Germany after German fashion. But the nearness of the Province to Gaul has taught the Gauls luxury, and so it has come to pass that the Gauls are not as good in battle as they used to be. It is interesting to gather from all these notices the progress of civilisation through the peoples of Europe, and some hint as to what has been thought to be good and bad for humanity by various races before the time of Christ.

Cæsar then tells us of a great Hercynian forest, beginning from the north of Switzerland and stretching away to the Danube. A man in nine days would traverse its breadth; but even in sixty days a man could not get to the end of it lengthwise. We may presume that the Black Forest was a portion of it. It contains many singular beasts,—bisons with one horn; elks, which are like great stags, but which have no joints in their legs, and cannot lie down,—nor, if knocked down, can they get up,—which sleep leaning against trees; but the trees sometimes break, and then the elk falls and has a bad time of it. Then there is the urus, almost as big as an elephant, which spares neither man nor beast. It is a great thing to kill a urus, but no one can tame them, even when young. The Germans are fond of mounting the horns of this animal with silver, and using them for drinking-cups.

Cæsar does very little over among the Germans. He comes back, partly destroys his bridge, and starts again in search of Ambiorix. His lieutenant Basilus nearly takes the poor hunted chieftain, but Ambiorix escapes, and Cæsar moralises about fortune. Ambiorix, the reader will remember, was joint-king over the Eburones with one Cativolcus. Cativolcus, who is old, finding how his people are harassed, curses his brother king who has brought these sorrows on the nation, and poisons himself with the juice of yew-tree.

All the tribes in the Belgic country, Gauls as well as Germans, were now very much harassed. They all had helped, or might have helped, or, if left to themselves, might at some future time give help to Ambiorix and the Eburones. Cæsar divides his army, but still goes himself in quest of his victim into the damp, uncomfortable countries near the mouths of the Scheldt and Meuse. Here he is much distracted between his burning desire to extirpate that race of wicked men over whom Ambiorix had been king, and his anxiety lest he should lose more of his own men in the work than the wicked race is worth. He invites the neighbouring Gauls to help him in the work, so that Gauls should perish in those inhospitable regions rather than his own legionaries. This, however, is fixed in his mind, that a tribe which has been guilty of so terrible an offence,—which has destroyed in war an army of his, just as he would have delighted to destroy a Gaulish army,—must be extirpated, so that its very name may cease to exist! "Pro tali facinore, stirps ac nomen civitatis tollatur."

Cæsar, in dividing his army, had stationed Q. Cicero with one legion and the heavy baggage and spoils of the army, in a fortress exactly at that spot from which Titurius Sabinus had been lured by the craft of Ambiorix. Certain Germans, the Sigambri, having learned that all the property of the Eburones had been given up by Cæsar as a prey to any who would take it, had crossed the Rhine that they might thus fill their hands. But it is suggested to them that they may fill their hands much fuller by attacking Q. Cicero in his camp; and they do attack him, when the best part of his army is away looking for provisions. That special spot in the territory of the Eburones is again nearly fatal to a Roman legion. But the Germans, not knowing how to press the advantage they gain, return with their spoil across the Rhine, and Cæsar again comes up like a god. But he has not as yet destroyed Ambiorix,—who indeed is not taken at last,—and expresses his great disgust and amazement that the coming of these Germans, which was planned with the view of injuring Ambiorix, should have done instead so great a service to that monstrously wicked chieftain.

He does his very best to catch Ambiorix in person, offering great rewards and inducing his men to undergo all manner of hardships in the pursuit. Ambiorix, however, with three or four chosen followers, escapes him. But Cæsar is not without revenge. He burns all the villages of the Eburones, and all their houses. He so lays waste the country that even when his army is gone not a soul should be able to live there. After that he probably allowed himself to be shaved. Ambiorix is seen here and is seen there, but with hairbreadth chances eludes his pursuer. Cæsar, having thus failed, returns south, as winter approaches, to Rheims,—Durocortorum; and just telling us in four words how he had one Acco tortured to death because Acco had headed a conspiracy in the middle of Gaul among the Carnutes and Senones, and how he outlawed and banished others whom he could not catch, he puts his legions into winter quarters, and again goes back to Italy to hold assizes and look after his interests amid the great affairs of the Republic.

CHAPTER VIII.

Seventh Book Of The War In Gaul.—The Revolt Of Vercingetorix.—B.C. 52.

In opening his account of his seventh campaign Cæsar makes almost the only
reference to the affairs of Rome which we find in these memoirs. Clodius has been
murdered. We know, too, that Crassus had been killed at the head of his army in
the east, and that, at the death of Clodius, Pompey had been created Dictator in
the city with the name of sole Consul. Cæsar, however, only mentions the murder
of Clodius, and then goes on to say that the Gauls, knowing how important to him
must be the affairs of Rome at this moment, think that he cannot now attend to
them, and that, in his absence, they may shake off the Roman yoke. The affairs of
Rome must indeed have been important to Cæsar, if, as no doubt is true, he had
already before his eyes a settled course of action by which to make himself supreme in the Republic. Clodius, the demagogue, was dead, whom he never could
have loved, but whom it had not suited him to treat as an enemy. Crassus, too,
was dead, whom, on account of his wealth, Cæsar had admitted as a colleague.
Pompey, the third triumvir, remained at Rome, and was now sole Consul; Pompey
who, only twelve months since, had so fondly given up his legion for the sake of
the Republic,—and for friendship. Cæsar, no doubt, foresaw by this time that the
struggle must be at last between himself and Pompey. The very forms of the old
republican rule were being turned adrift, and Cæsar must have known, as Pompey
also knew, and Clodius had known, and even Crassus, that a new power would
become paramount in the city. But the hands to wrest such power must be very
strong. And the day had not yet quite come. Having spent six summers in subdu-
ing Gaul, Cæsar would not lose the prestige, the power, the support, which such
a territory, really subdued, would give him. Things, doubtless, were important at
Rome, but it was still his most politic course to return over the Alps and complete
his work. Before the winter was over he heard that the tribes were conspiring, because it was thought that at such an emergency Cæsar could not leave Italy.

This last book of the Commentary, as written by Cæsar, tells the story of the
gallant Vercingetorix, one of the Arverni,—the modern Auvergne,—whose father,
Celtillus, is said to have sought the chieftainship of all Gaul, and to have been killed
on that account by his own state. Vercingetorix is certainly the hero of these wars
on the Gaulish side, though we hear nothing of him till this seventh campaign.
The conspiracy against Rome is afloat, the Carnutes, whose chief town is Genabum,—Orleans,—having commenced it. Vercingetorix excites his own countrymen
to join, but is expelled from their town, Gergovia, for the attempt. The Arverni,

or at least their chief men, fear to oppose the Romans; but Vercingetorix obtains a crowd of followers out in the country, and perseveres. Men of other tribes come to him, from as far north as Paris, and west from the Ocean. He assumes supreme power, and enacts and carries out most severe laws for his guidance during the war. For any greater offence he burns the offender alive and subjects him to all kinds of torments. For any small fault he cuts off a man's ears, pokes out one of his eyes, and sends him home, that he may be an example visible to all men. By threats of such punishment to those who do not join him, and by inflicting such on those who do and are then untrue to him or lukewarm, he gets together a great army. Cæsar, who is still in Italy, hears of all this, and having made things comfortable with Pompey, hurries into the province. He tells us of his great difficulty in joining his army,—of the necessity which is incumbent on him of securing even the Roman Province from invasion, and of the manner in which he breaks through snow-clad mountains, the Cevennes, at a time of the year in which such mountains were supposed to be impassable. He is forced into fighting before the winter is over, because, unless he does so, the few friends he has in Gaul,—the Ædui, for instance,—will have been gained over by the enemy. This made it very difficult, Cæsar tells us, for him to know what to do; but he decides that he must begin his campaign, though it be winter still.

Cæsar, moving his army about with wonderful quickness, takes three towns in the centre of Gaul, of which Genabum, Orleans, is the first, and thus provides himself with food. Vercingetorix, when he hears of these losses, greatly troubled in his mind that Cæsar should thus he enabled to exist on the provisions gathered by the Gauls, determines to burn all the Gaulish towns in those parts. He tells his people that there is nothing else for them in their present emergency, and that they must remember when they see their hearths smoking and their property destroyed, that it would be, or ought to be, much more grievous for them to know that their wives and children would become slaves, as undoubtedly would be their fate, if Cæsar were allowed to prevail. The order is given. Twenty cities belonging to one tribe are burned to the ground. The same thing is done in other states. But there is one very beautiful city, the glory of the country round, which can, they say, be so easily defended that it will be a comfort rather than a peril to them. Avaricum, the present Bourges,—must that also be burned? May not Avaricum be spared? Vercingetorix is all for burning Avaricum as he has burned the others; but he allows himself to be persuaded, and the city is spared—for the time.

Cæsar, of course, determines to take Avaricum; but he encounters great difficulties. The cattle have been driven away. There is no corn. Those wretched Ædui do almost nothing for him; and the Boii, who are their neighbours, and who, at the best, are but a poor scanty people, are equally unserviceable. Some days his army is absolutely without food; but yet no word of complaint is heard "unworthy of the majesty and former victories of the Roman people." The soldiers even beg him to continue the siege when he offers to raise it because of the hardships they are enduring. Let them endure anything, they say, but failure! "Moreover Cæsar, when he would accost his legions one by one at their work, and would tell them that he would raise the siege if they could but ill bear their privations, was implored by all of them not to do that. They said that for many years under his command they had so well done their duty that they had undergone no disgrace, had never quitted their ground leaving aught unfinished,"—except the subjugation of Britain they might perhaps have said,—"that they would be now disgraced if they should raise a siege which had been commenced; that they would rather bear all hardships than not avenge the Roman citizens who had perished at Genabum by the perfidy of the Gauls." Cæsar puts these words into the mouths of his legionaries, and as we read them we believe that such was the existing spirit of the men. Cæsar's soldiers now had learned better than to cry because they were afraid of their enemies.

Then we hear that Vercingetorix is in trouble with the Gauls. The Gauls, when they see the Romans so near them, think that they are to be betrayed into Cæsar's hands, and they accuse their leader. But Vercingetorix makes them a speech, and brings up certain Roman prisoners to give evidence as to the evil condition of the Roman army. Vercingetorix swears that these prisoners are soldiers from the Roman legions, and so settles that little trouble; but Cæsar, defending his legionaries, asserts that the men so used were simply slaves.

Vercingetorix is in his camp at some little distance from Avaricum, while Cæsar is determined to take the city. We have the description of the siege, concise, graphic, and clear. We are told of the nature of the walls; how the Gauls were good at mining and countermining; how they flung hot pitch and boiling grease on the invaders; how this was kept up, one Gaul after another stepping on to the body of his dying comrade; how at last they resolved to quit the town and make their way by night to the camp of Vercingetorix, but were stopped by the prayers of their own women, who feared Cæsar's mercies;—and how at last the city was taken. We cannot but execrate Cæsar when he tells us coolly of the result. They were all killed. The old, the women, and the children, perished altogether, slaughtered by the Romans. Out of forty thousand inhabitants, Cæsar says that about eight hundred got safely to Vercingetorix. Of course we doubt the accuracy of Cæsar's figures when he tells us of the numbers of the Gauls; but we do not doubt that but a few escaped, and that all but a few were slaughtered. When, during the last campaign, the Gauls at Genabum (Orleans) had determined on revolt against Cæsar, certain Roman traders—usurers for the most part, who had there established themselves—were killed. Cæsar gives this as the cause, and sufficient cause, for the wholesale slaughter of women and children! One reflects that not otherwise, perhaps, could he have conquered Gaul, and that Gaul had to be conquered; but we cannot for the moment but abhor the man capable of such work. Vercingetorix bears his loss bravely. He reminds the Gauls that had they taken his advice the city would have been destroyed by themselves and not defended; he tells them that all the states of Gaul are now ready to join him; and he prepares to fortify a camp after the Roman fashion. Hitherto the Gauls have fought either from behind the walls of towns, or out in the open country without other protection than that of the woods and hills.

Then there is another episode with those unsatisfactory Ædui. There is a quarrel among them who shall be their chief magistrate,—a certain old man or a certain young man,—and they send to Cæsar to settle the question. Cæsar's hands are very full; but, as he explains, it is essential to him that his allies shall be kept in due subordinate order. He therefore absolutely goes in person to one of their cities, and decides that the young man shall be the chief magistrate. But, as he seldom does anything for nothing, he begs that ten thousand Æduan infantry and all the Æduan cavalry may be sent to help him against Vercingetorix. The Ædui have no alternative but to comply. Their compliance, however, is not altogether of a friendly nature. The old man who has been put out of the magistracy gets hold of the Æduan general of the forces; and the Æduan army takes the field,—to help, not Cæsar, but Vercingetorix! There is a large amount of lying and treachery among the Ædui, and of course tidings of what is going on are carried to Cæsar. Over and over again these people deceive him, betray him, and endeavour to injure his cause; but he always forgives them, or pretends to forgive them. It is his policy to show to the Gauls how great can be the friendship and clemency of Cæsar. If he would have burned the Ædui and spared Bourges we should have liked him better; but then, had he done so, he would not have been Cæsar.

While Cæsar is thus troubled with his allies, he has trouble enough also with his enemies. Vercingetorix, with his followers, after that terrible reverse at Avaricum,—Bourges,—goes into his own country which we know as Auvergne, and there encamps his army on a high hill with a flat top, called Gergovia. All of us who have visited Clermont have probably seen the hill. Vercingetorix makes three camps for his army on the hill, and the Arverni have a town there. The Gaul has so placed himself that there shall be a river not capable of being forded between himself and Cæsar. But the Roman general makes a bridge and sets himself down with his legions before Gergovia. The limits of this little work do not admit of any detailed description of Cæsar's battles; but perhaps there is none more interesting than this siege. The three Gaulish camps are taken. The women of Gergovia, thinking that their town is taken also, leaning over the walls, implore mercy from the Romans, and beg that they may not be treated as have the women of Avaricum. Certain leading Roman soldiers absolutely climb up into the town. The reader also thinks that Cæsar is to prevail, as he always does prevail. But he is beaten back, and has to give it up. On this occasion the gallant Vercingetorix is the master of the day, and Cæsar excuses himself by explaining how it was that his legions were defeated through the rash courage of his own men, and not by bad generalship of his own. And it probably was so. The reader always feels inclined to believe the Commentary, even when he may most dislike Cæsar. Cæsar again makes his bridge over the river, the Allier, and retires into the territory of his doubtful friends the Ædui. He tells us himself that in that affair he lost 700 men and 46 officers.

It seems that at this time Cæsar with his whole army must have been in great danger of being destroyed by the Gauls. Why Vercingetorix did not follow up his victory and prevent Cæsar from escaping over the Allier is not explained. No doubt the requirements of warfare were not known to the Gaul as they were to the Roman. As it was, Cæsar had enough to do to save his army. The Ædui, of course, turned against him again. All his stores and treasure and baggage were at Noviodunum,—Nevers,—a town belonging to the Ædui. These are seized by his allies, who destroy all that they cannot carry away, and Cæsar's army is in danger of being starved. Everything has been eaten up where he is, and the Loire, without bridges or fords, was between him and a country where food was to be found. He does cross the river, the Ædui having supposed that it would be impossible. He finds a spot in which his men can wade across with their shoulders just above the waters. Bad as the spot is for fording, in his great difficulty he makes the attempt and accomplishes it.

Then there is an account of a battle which Labienus is obliged to fight up near Paris. He has four legions away with him there, and having heard of Cæsar's misfortune at Gergovia, knows how imperative it is that he should join his chief. He fights his battle and wins it, and Cæsar tells the story quite as enthusiastically as though he himself had been the conqueror. When this difficulty is overcome, Labienus comes south and joins his Imperator.

The Gauls are still determined to drive Cæsar out of their country, and with this object call together a great council at Bibracte, which was the chief town of the Ædui. It was afterwards called Augustodunum, which has passed into the modern name Autun. At this meeting, the Ædui, who, having been for some years past bolstered up by Rome, think themselves the first of all the Gauls, demand that the chief authority in the revolt against Rome,—now that they have revolted,—shall be intrusted to them. An Æduan chief, they think, should be the commander-in-chief in this war against Rome. Who has done so much for the revolt as the Ædui, who have thrown over their friends the Romans,—now for about the tenth time? But Vercingetorix is unanimously elected, and the Æduan chiefs are disgusted. Then there is another battle. Vercingetorix thinks that he is strong enough to attack the enemy as Cæsar is going down south towards the Province. Cæsar, so says Vercingetorix, is in fact retreating. And, indeed, it seems that Cæsar was retreating. But the Gauls are beaten and fly, losing some three thousand of their men who are slaughtered in the fight. Vercingetorix shuts himself up in a town called Alesia, and Cæsar prepares for another siege.

The taking of Alesia is the last event told in Cæsar's Commentary on the Gallic War, and of all the stories told, it is perhaps the most heartrending. Civilisation was never forwarded in a fashion more terrible than that which prevailed at this siege. Vercingetorix with his whole army is forced into the town, and Cæsar surrounds it with ditches, works, lines, and ramparts, so that no one shall be able to escape from it. Before this is completed, and while there is yet a way open of leaving the town, the Gaulish chief sends out horsemen, who are to go to all the tribes of Gaul, and convene the fighting men to that place, so that by their numbers they may raise the siege and expel the Romans. We find that these horsemen do as they are bidden, and that a great Gaulish conference is held, at which it is decided how many men shall be sent by each tribe. Vercingetorix has been very touching in his demand that all this shall be done quickly. He has food for the town for thirty days. Probably it may be stretched to last a little longer. Then, if the tribes are not true to him, he and the eighty thousand souls he has with him must perish. The horsemen make good their escape from the town, and Vercingetorix, with his eighty thousand hungry souls around him, prepares to wait. It seems to us, when we think what must have been the Gallia of those days, and when we remember how far thirty days would now be for sufficing for such a purpose, that the difficulties to be overcome were insuperable. But Cæsar says that the tribes did send their men, each tribe sending the number demanded, except the Bellovaci,—the men of Beauvais,—who declared that they chose to wage war on their own account; but even they, out of kindness, lent two thousand men. Cæsar explains that even his own best friends among the Gauls,—among whom was one Commius, who had been very useful to him in Britain, and whom he had made king over his own tribe, the Atrebates,—at this conjuncture of affairs felt themselves bound to join the national movement. This Commius had even begged for the two thousand men of Beauvais. So great, says Cæsar, was the united desire of Gaul to recover Gallic liberty, that they were deterred from coming by no memory of benefits or of friendship. Eight thousand horsemen and two hundred and forty thousand footmen assembled themselves in the territories of the Ædui. Alesia was north of the Ædui, amidst the Lingones. This enormous army chose its generals, and marched off to Alesia to relieve Vercingetorix.

But the thirty days were past, and more than past, and the men and women in Alesia were starving. No tidings ever had reached Alesia of the progress which was being made in the gathering of their friends. It had come to be very bad with them there. Some were talking of unconditional surrender. Others proposed to cut their way through the Roman lines. Then one Critognatus had a suggestion to make, and Cæsar gives us the words of his speech. It has been common with the Greek and Latin historians to put speeches into the mouths of certain orators, adding the words when the matter has come within either their knowledge or belief. Cæsar does not often thus risk his credibility; but on this occasion he does so. We have the speech of Critognatus, word for word. Of those who speak of surrender he thinks so meanly that he will not notice them. As to that cutting a way through the Roman lines, which means death, he is of opinion that to endure misfortune is greater than to die. Many a man can die who cannot bravely live and suffer. Let them endure a little longer. Why doubt the truth and constancy of the tribes? Then he makes his suggestion. Let those who can fight, and are thus useful,—eat those who are useless and cannot fight; and thus live till the levies of all Gaul shall have come to their succour! Those who have authority in Alesia cannot quite bring themselves to this, but they do that which is horrible in the next degree. They will turn out of the town all the old, all the weak, and all the women. After that,—if that will not suffice,—then they will begin to eat each other. The town belongs, or did belong, to a people called the Mandubii,—not to Vercingetorix or his tribe; and the Mandubii, with their children and women, are compelled to go out.

But whither shall they go? Cæsar has told us that there was a margin of ground between his lines and the city wall,—an enclosed space from which there was no egress except into Cæsar's camp or into the besieged town. Here stand these weak ones,—aged men, women, and children,—and implore Cæsar to receive them into his camp, so that they may pass out into the open country. There they stood as supplicants, on that narrow margin of ground between two armies. Their own friends, having no food for them, had expelled them from their own homes. Would Cæsar have mercy? Cæsar, with a wave of his hand, declines to have mercy. He tells us what he himself decides to do in eight words. "At Cæsar, depositis in vallo custodiis, recipi prohibebat." "But Cæsar, having placed guards along the rampart, forbade that they should be received." We hear no more of them, but we know that they perished!

The collected forces of Gaul do at last come up to attempt the rescue of Vercingetorix,—and indeed they come in time; were they able by coming to do anything? They attack Cæsar in his camp, and a great battle is fought beneath the eyes of the men in Alesia. But Cæsar is very careful that those who now are hemmed up in the town shall not join themselves to the Gauls who had spread over the country all around him. We hear how during the battle Cæsar comes up himself, and is known by the colour of his cloak. We again feel, as we read his account of the fighting, that the Gauls nearly win, and that they ought to win. But at last they are driven headlong in flight,—all the levies of all the tribes. The Romans kill very many: were not the labour of killing too much for them, they might kill all. A huge crowd, however, escapes, and the men scatter themselves back into their tribes.

On the next day Vercingetorix yields himself and the city to Cæsar. During the late battle he and his men shut up within the walls have been simply spectators of the fighting. Cæsar is sitting in his lines before his camp; and there the chieftains, with Vercingetorix at their head, are brought up to him. Plutarch tells us a story of the chieftain riding up before Cæsar, to deliver himself, with gilt armour, on a grand horse, caracolling and prancing. We cannot fancy that any horse out of Alesia, could, after the siege, have been fit for such holiday occasion. The horses out of Vercingetorix's stables had probably been eaten many days since. Then Cæsar again forgives the Ædui; but Vercingetorix is taken as a prisoner to Rome, is kept a prisoner for six years, is then led in Cæsar's Triumph, and, after these six years, is destroyed, as a victim needed for Cæsar's glory,—that so honour may be done to Cæsar! Cæsar puts his army into winter quarters, and determines to remain himself in Gaul during the winter. When his account of these things reaches Home, a "supplication" of twenty days is decreed in his honour.

This is the end of Cæsar's Commentary "De Bello Gallico." The war was carried on for two years more; and a memoir of Cæsar's doings during those two years,—B.C. 51 and 50,—was written, after Cæsar's manner, by one Aulus Hirtius. There is no pretence on the writer's part that this was the work of Cæsar's hands, as in a short preface he makes an author's apology for venturing to continue what Cæsar had begun. The most memorable circumstance of Cæsar's warfares told in this record of two campaigns is the taking of Uxellodunum, a town in the southwest of France, the site of which is not now known. Cæsar took the town by cutting off the water, and then horribly mutilated the inhabitants who had dared to defend their own hearths. "Cæsar," says this historian, "knowing well that his clemency was acknowledged by all men, and that he need not fear that any punishment inflicted by him would be attributed to the cruelty of his nature, perceiving also that he could never know what might be the end of his policy if such rebellions should continue to break out, thought that other Gauls should be deterred by the fear of punishment." So he cut off the hands of all those who had borne arms at Uxellodunum, and turned the maimed wretches adrift upon the world! And his apologist adds, that he gave them life so that the punishment of these wicked ones,—who had fought for their liberty,—might be the more manifest to the world at large! This was perhaps the crowning act of Cæsar's cruelty,—defended, as we see, by the character he had achieved for clemency!

Soon after this Gaul was really subdued, and then we hear the first preparatory notes of the coming civil war. An attempt was made at Rome to ruin Cæsar in his absence. One of the consuls of the year,—B.C. 51,—endeavoured to deprive him of the remainder of the term of his proconsulship, and to debar him from seeking the suffrages of the people for the consulship in his absence. Two of his legions are also demanded from him, and are surrendered by him. The order, indeed, is for one legion from him and one from Pompeius; but he has had with him, as the reader will remember, a legion borrowed from Pompeius;—and thus in fact Cæsar is called upon to give up two legions. And he gives them up,—not being as yet quite ready to pass the Rubicon.

CHAPTER IX.

First Book Of The Civil War.—Cæsar Crosses The Rubicon.—Follows Pompey To Brundusium.—And Conquers Afranius In Spain.—B.C. 49.

Cæsar now gives us his history of that civil war in which he and Pompey contended for the mastery over Rome and the Republic. In his first Commentary he had recorded his campaigns in Gaul,—campaigns in which he reduced tribes which were, if not hostile, at any rate foreign, and by his success in which he carried on and maintained the potency, traditions, and purport of the Roman Republic. It was the ambition of the Roman to be master of the known world. In his ideas no more of the world was really known than had become Roman, and any extension to the limits of this world could only be made by the addition of so-called barbarous tribes to the number of Roman subjects. In reducing Gaul, therefore, and in fighting with the Germans, and in going over to Britain, Cæsar was doing that which all good Romans wished to see done, and was rivalling in the West the great deeds which Pompey had accomplished for the Republic in the East. In this second Commentary he is forced to deal with a subject which must have been less gratifying to Roman readers. He relates to us the victories which he won with Roman legions over other legions equally Roman, and by which he succeeded in destroying the liberty of the Republic.

It must he acknowledged on Cæsar's behalf that in truth liberty had fallen in Rome before Cæsar's time. Power had produced wealth, and wealth had produced corruption. The tribes of Rome were bought and sold at the various elections, and a few great oligarchs, either of this faction or of that, divided among themselves the places of trust and honour and power, and did so with hands ever open for the grasping of public wealth. An honest man with clean hands and a conscience, with scruples and a love of country, became unfitted for public employment. Cato in these days was simply ridiculous; and even Cicero, though he was a trimmer, was too honest for the times. Laws were wrested from their purposes, and the very Tribunes[11] of the people had become the worst of tyrants. It was necessary, perhaps, that there should be a master;—so at least Cæsar thought. He had, no doubt, seen this necessity during all these years of fighting in Gaul, and had resolved that he would not be less than First in the new order of things. So he crossed the Rubicon.

---

[11] The Tribunes of the people were officers elected annually to act on behalf of the people as checks on the magistracy of the Republic, and were endowed with vast powers, which they were presumed to use for the protection of liberty. But the office of Tribune had become degraded to party purposes, as had every other office of the state.

The reader of this second Commentary will find it less alluring than the first. There is less in it of adventure, less of new strange life, and less of that sound, healthy, joyous feeling which sprang from a thorough conviction on Cæsar's part that in crushing the Gauls he was doing a thoroughly good thing. To us, and our way of thinking, his doings in Gaul were stained with terrible cruelty. To him and to his Romans they were foul with no such stain. How other Roman conquerors acted to other conquered peoples we may learn from the fact, that Cæsar obtained a character for great mercy by his forbearance in Gaul. He always writes as though he were free from any sting of conscience, as he tells us of the punishments which policy called upon him to inflict. But as he writes of these civil wars, there is an absence of this feeling of perfect self-satisfaction, and at the same time he is much less cruel. Hecatombs of Gauls, whether men or women or children, he could see burned or drowned or starved, mutilated or tortured, without a shudder. He could give the command for such operations with less remorse than we feel when we order the destruction of a litter of undesirable puppies. But he could not bring himself to slay Roman legionaries, even in fair fighting, with anything like self-satisfaction. In this he was either soft-hearted or had a more thorough feeling of country than generals or soldiers who have fought in civil contests since his time have shown. In the Wars of the Roses and in those of Cromwell we recognise no such feeling. The American generals were not so restrained. But Cæsar seems to have valued a Roman legionary more than a tribe of Gauls.

Nevertheless he crossed the Rubicon. We have all heard of this crossing of the Rubicon, but Cæsar says nothing about it. The Rubicon was a little river, now almost if not altogether unknown, running into the Adriatic between Ravenna and Ariminum, — Rimini, — and dividing the provinces of so-called Cisalpine Gaul from the territory under the immediate rule of the magistracy of Rome. Cæsar was, so to say, at home north of the Rubicon. He was in his own province, and had all things under his command. But he was forbidden by the laws even to enter the territory of Rome proper while in the command of a Roman province; and therefore, in crossing the Rubicon, he disobeyed the laws, and put himself in opposition to the constituted authorities of the city. It does not appear, however, that very much was thought of this, or that the passage of the river was in truth taken as the special sign of Cæsar's purpose, or as a deed that was irrevocable in its consequences. There are various pretty stories of Cæsar's hesitation as he stood on the brink of the river, doubting whether he would plunge the world into civil war. We are told how a spirit appeared to him and led him across the water with martial music, and how Cæsar, declaring that the die was cast, went on and crossed the fatal stream. But all this was fable, invented on Cæsar's behalf by Romans who came after Cæsar. Cæsar's purpose was, no doubt, well understood when he brought one of his legions down into that corner of his province, but offers to treat with him on friendly terms were made by Pompey and his party after he had established himself on the Roman side of the river.

When the civil war began, Cæsar had still, according to the assignment made to him, two years and a half left of his allotted period of government in the three provinces; but his victories and his power had been watched with anxious eyes from Rome, and the Senate had attempted to decree that he should be recalled. Pompey was no longer Cæsar's friend, nor did Cæsar expect his friendship. Pompey, who had lately played his cards but badly, and must have felt that he had played them badly, had been freed from his bondage to Cæsar by the death of Crassus, the third triumvir, by the death of Julia, Cæsar's daughter, and by the course of things in Rome. It had been an unnatural alliance arranged by Cæsar with the view of clipping his rival's wings. The fortunes of Pompey had hitherto been so bright, that he also had seemed to be divine. While still a boy, he had commanded and conquered, women had adored him, the soldiers had worshipped him. Sulla had called him the Great; and, as we are told, had raised his hat to him in token of honour. He had been allowed the glory of a Triumph while yet a youth, and had triumphed a second time before he had reached middle life. He had triumphed again a third time, and the three Triumphs had been won in the three quarters of the globe. In all things he had been successful, and in all things happy. He had driven the swarming pirates from every harbour in the Mediterranean, and had filled Rome with corn. He had returned a conqueror with his legions from the East, and had dared to disband them, that he might live again as a private citizen. And after that, when it was thought necessary that the city should be saved, in her need, from the factions of her own citizens, he had been made sole consul. It is easier now to understand the character of Pompey than the position which, by his unvaried successes, he had made for himself in the minds both of the nobles and of the people. Even up to this time, even after Cæsar's wars in Gaul, there was something of divinity hanging about Pompey, in which the Romans of the city trusted. He had been imperious, but calm in manner and self-possessed,—allowing no one to be his equal, but not impatient in making good his claims; grand, handsome, lavish when policy required it, rapacious when much was needed, never self-indulgent, heartless, false, cruel, politic, ambitious, very brave, and a Roman to the backbone. But he had this failing, this weakness;—when the time for the last struggle came, he did not quite know what it was that he desired to do; he did not clearly see his future. The things to be done were so great, that he had not ceased to doubt concerning them when the moment came in which doubt was fatal. Cæsar saw it all, and never doubted. That little tale of Cæsar standing on the bridge over the Rubicon pondering as to his future course,—divided between obedience and rebellion,—is very pretty. But there was no such pondering, and no such division. Cæsar knew very well what he meant and what he wanted.

Cæsar is full of his wrongs as he begins his second narrative. He tells us how his own friends are silenced in the Senate and in the city; how his enemies, Scipio, Cato, and Lentulus the consul, prevail; how no one is allowed to say a word for him. "Pompey himself," he says, "urged on by the enemies of Cæsar, and because he was unwilling that any one should equal himself in honour, had turned himself altogether from Cæsar's friendship, and had gone back to the fellowship of their common enemies,—enemies whom he himself had created for Cæsar during the time of their alliance. At the same time, conscious of the scandal of those two legions which he had stopped on their destined road to Asia and Syria and taken into his own hand, he was anxious that the question should be referred to arms." Those two legions are very grievous to Cæsar. One was the legion, which, as we remember, Pompey had given up to friendship,—and the Republic. When, in the beginning of these contests between the two rivals, the Senate had decided on weakening each by demanding from each a legion, Pompey had asked Cæsar for the restitution of that which he had so kindly lent. Cæsar, too proud to refuse payment of the debt, had sent that to his former friend, and had also sent another legion, as demanded, to the Senate. They were required nominally for service in the East, and now were in the hands of him who had been Cæsar's friend but had become his enemy. It is no wonder that Cæsar talks of the infamy or scandal of the two legions! He repeats his complaint as to the two legions again and again.

In the month of January Cæsar was at Ravenna, just north of the Rubicon, and in his own province. Messages pass between him and the Senate, and he proposes his terms. The Senate also proposes its terms. He must lay down his arms, or he will be esteemed an enemy by the Republic. All Rome is disturbed. The account is Cæsar's account, but we imagine that Rome was disturbed. "Soldiers are recruited over all Italy; arms are demanded, taxes are levied on the municipalities, and money is taken from the sacred shrines; all laws divine and human are disregarded." Then Cæsar explains to his soldiers his wrongs, and the crimes of Pompey. He tells them how they, under his guidance, have been victorious, how under him they have "pacified" all Gaul and Germany, and he calls upon them to defend him who has enabled them to do such great things. He has but one legion with him, but that legion declares that it will obey him,—him and the tribunes of the people, some of whom, acting on Cæsar's side, have come over from Rome to Ravenna. We can appreciate the spirit of this allusion to the tribunes, so that there may seem to be still some link between Cæsar and the civic authorities. When the soldiers have expressed their goodwill, he goes to Ariminum, and so the Rubicon is passed.

There are still more messages. Cæsar expresses himself as greatly grieved that he should be subjected to so much suspense, nevertheless he is willing to suffer anything for the Republic;—"omnia pati reipublicæ causâ." Only let Pompey go to his province, let the legions in and about Rome be disbanded, let all the old forms of free government be restored, and panic be abolished, and then,—when that is done,—all difficulties may be settled in a few minutes' talking. The consuls and Pompey send back word that if Cæsar will go back into Gaul and dismiss his army, Pompey shall go at once to Spain. But Pompey and the consuls with their troops will not stir till Cæsar shall have given security for his departure. Each demands that the other shall first abandon his position. Of course all these messages mean nothing.

Cæsar, complaining bitterly of injustice, sends a portion of his small army still farther into the Roman territory. Marc Antony goes to Arezzo with five cohorts, and Cæsar occupies three other cities with a cohort each. The marvel is that he was not attacked and driven back by Pompey. We may probably conclude that the soldiers, though under the command of Pompey, were not trustworthy as against Cæsar. As Cæsar regrets his two legions, so no doubt do the two legions regret their commander. At any rate, the consular forces with Pompey and the consuls and a host of senators retreat southwards to Brundusium,—Brindisi,—intending to leave Italy by the port which we shall all use before long when we go eastwards.

During this retreat, the first blood in the civil war is spilt at Corfinium, a town which, if it now stood at all, would stand in the Abruzzi. Cæsar there is victor in a small engagement, and obtains possession of the town. The Pompeian officers whom he finds there he sends away, and allows them even to carry with them money which he believes to have been taken from the public treasury. Throughout his route southward the soldiers of Pompey,—who had heretofore been his soldiers,—return to him. Pompey and the consuls still retreat, and still Cæsar follows them, though Pompey had boasted, when first warned to beware of Cæsar, that he had only to stamp upon Italian soil and legions would arise from the earth ready to obey him. He knows, however, that away from Rome, in her provinces, in Macedonia and Achaia, in Asia and Cilicia, in Sicily, Sardinia, and Africa, in Mauritania and the two Spains, there are Roman legions which as yet know no Cæsar. It may be better for Pompey that he should stamp his foot somewhere out of Italy. At any rate he sends the obedient consuls and his attendant senators over to Dyrrachium in Illyria with a part of his army, and follows with the remainder as soon as Cæsar is at his heels. Cæsar makes an effort to intercept him and his fleet, but in that he fails. Thus Pompey deserts Rome and Italy,—and never again sees the imperial city or the fair land.

Cæsar explains to us why he does not follow his enemy and endeavour at once to put an end to the struggle. Pompey is provided with shipping and he is not; and he is aware that the force of Rome lies in her provinces. Moreover, Rome may be starved by Pompey, unless he, Cæsar, can take care that the corn-growing countries, which are the granaries of Rome, are left free for the use of the city. He must make sure of the two Gauls, and of Sardinia, and of Sicily, of Africa too, if it may be possible. He must win to his cause the two Spains, of which at least the northern province was at present devoted to Pompey. He sends one lieutenant to Sardinia with a legion, another to Sicily with three legions,—and from Sicily over into Africa. These provinces had been allotted to partisans of Pompey; but Cæsar is successful with them all. To Cato, the virtuous man, had been assigned the government of Sicily; but Cato finds no Pompeian army ready for his use, and, complaining bitterly that he has been deceived and betrayed by the head of his faction, runs away, and leaves his province to Cæsar's officers. Cæsar determines that he himself will carry the war into Spain.

But he found it necessary first to go to Rome, and Cæsar, in his account of what he did there, hardly tells us the whole truth. We quite go along with him when he explains to us that, having collected what sort of a Senate he could,—for Pompey had taken away with him such senators as he could induce to follow him,—and having proposed to this meagre Senate that ambassadors should be sent to Pompey, the Senate accepted his suggestion; but that nobody could be induced to go on such an errand. Pompey had already declared that all who remained at Rome were his enemies. And it may probably be true that Cæsar, as he says, found a certain tribune of the people at Rome who opposed him in all that he was doing, though we should imagine that the opposition was not violent. But his real object in going to Rome was to lay hand on the treasure of the Republic,—the sanctius ærarium,—which was kept in the temple of Saturn for special emergencies of State. That he should have taken this we do not wonder;—but we do wonder that he should have taken the trouble to say that he did not do so. He professes that he was so hindered by that vexatious tribune, that he could not accomplish the purposes for which he had come. But he certainly did take the money, and we cannot doubt but that he went to Rome especially to get it.

Cæsar, on his way to Spain, goes to Marseilles, which, under the name of Massilia, was at this time, as it is now, the most thriving mercantile port on the Mediterranean. It belonged to the province of Further Gaul, but it was in fact a colony of Greek traders. Its possession was now necessary to Cæsar. The magistrates of the town, when called upon for their adhesion, gave a most sensible answer. They protest that they are very fond of Cæsar, and very fond of Pompey. They don't understand all these affairs of Rome, and regret that two such excellent men should quarrel. In the mean time they prefer to hold their own town. Cæsar speaks of this decision as an injury to himself, and is instigated by such wrongs against him to besiege the city, which he does both by land and sea, leaving officers there for the purpose, and going on himself to Spain.

At this time all Spain was held by three officers, devoted to the cause of Pompey, though, from what has gone before, it is clear that Cæsar fears nothing from the south. Afranius commanded in the north and east, holding the southern spurs of the Pyrenees. Petreius, who was stationed in Lusitania, in the south-west, according to agreement, hurries up to the assistance of Afranius as soon as Cæsar approaches. The Pompeian and Cæsarian armies are brought into close quarters in the neighbourhood of Ilerda (Lerida), on the little river Sicoris, or Segre, which runs into the Ebro. They are near the mountains here, and the nature of the fighting is controlled by the rapidity and size of the rivers, and the inequality of the ground. Cæsar describes the campaign with great minuteness, imparting to it a wonderful interest by the clearness of his narrative. Afranius and Petreius hold the town of Ilerda, which is full of provisions. Cæsar is very much pressed by want, as the corn and grass have not yet grown, and the country supplies of the former year are almost exhausted. So great are his difficulties, that tidings reach Rome that Afranius has conquered him. Hearing this, many who were still clinging to the city, doubtful as to the side they would take, go away to Pompey. But Cæsar at last manages to make Ilerda too hot for the Pompeian generals. He takes his army over one river in coracles, such as he had seen in Britain; he turns the course of another; fords a third, breaking the course of the stream by the bulk of his horses; and bridges a fourth. Afranius and Petreius find that they must leave Ilerda, and escape over the Ebro among the half-barbarous tribe further south, and make their way, if possible, among the Celtibri,—getting out of Aragon into Castile, as the division was made in after-ages. Cæsar gives us as one reason for this intended march on the part of his enemies, that Pompey was well known by those tribes, but that the name of Cæsar was a name as yet obscure to the barbarians. It was not, however, easy for Afranius to pass over the Ebro without Cæsar's leave, and Cæsar will by no means give him leave. He intercepts the Pompeians, and now turns upon them that terrible engine of want from which he had suffered so much. He continues so to drive them about, still north of the Ebro, that they can get at no water; and at last they are compelled to surrender.

During the latter days of this contest the Afranians, as they are called—Roman legionaries, as are the soldiers of Cæsar—fraternise with their brethren in Cæsar's camp, and there is something of free intercourse between the two Roman armies. The upshot is that the soldiers of Afranius resolve to give themselves up to Cæsar, bargaining, however, that their own generals shall be secure. Afranius is willing enough; but his brother-general, Petreius, with more of the Roman at heart, will not hear of it. We shall hear hereafter the strange fate of this Petreius. He stops the conspiracy with energy, and forces from his own men, and even from Afranius, an oath against surrender. He orders that all Cæsar's soldiers found in their camp shall be killed, and, as Cæsar tells us, brings back the affair to the old form of war. But it is all of no avail. The Afranians are so driven by the want of water, that the two generals are at last compelled to capitulate and lay down their arms.

Five words which are used by Cæsar in the description of this affair give us a strong instance of his conciseness in the use of words, and of the capability for conciseness which the Latin language affords. "Premebantur Afraniani pabulatione, aquabantur ægre." "The soldiers of Afranius were much distressed in the matter of forage, and could obtain water only with great difficulty." These twenty words translate those five which Cæsar uses, perhaps with fair accuracy; but many more than twenty would probably have been used by any English historian in dealing with the same facts.

Cæsar treats his compatriots with the utmost generosity. So many conquered Gauls he would have sold as slaves, slaughtering their leaders, or he would have cut off their hands, or have driven them down upon the river and have allowed them to perish in the waters. But his conquered foes are Roman soldiers, and he simply demands that the army of Afranius shall be disbanded, and that the leaders of it shall go,—whither they please. He makes them a speech in which he explains how badly they have treated him. Nevertheless he will hurt no one. He has borne it all, and will bear it, patiently. Let the generals only leave the Province, and let the army which they have led be disbanded. He will not keep a soldier who does not wish to stay with him, and will even pay those whom Afranius has been unable to pay out of his own funds. Those who have houses and land in Spain may remain there. Those who have none he will first feed and afterwards take back, if not to Italy, at any rate to the borders of Italy. The property which his own soldiers have taken from them in the chances of war shall be restored, and he out of his own pocket will compensate his own men. He performs his promise, and takes all those who do not choose to remain, to the banks of the Var, which divides the Province from Italy, and there sets them down, full, no doubt, of gratitude to their conqueror. Never was there such clemency,—or, we may say, better policy! Cæsar's whole campaign in Spain had occupied him only forty days.

In the mean time Decimus Brutus, to whom we remember that Cæsar had given the command of the ships which he prepared against the Veneti in the west of Gaul, and who was hereafter to be one of those who slew him in the Capitol, obtains a naval victory over the much more numerous fleet of the Massilians. They had prepared seventeen big ships,—"naves longæ" they are called by Cæsar,—

and of these Brutus either destroys or takes nine. In his next book Cæsar proceeds to tell us how things went on at Marseilles both by sea and land after this affair.

CHAPTER X.

Second Book Of The Civil War.—The Taking Of Marseilles.—Varro In
The South Of Spain.—The Fate Of Curio Before Utica.—B.C. 49.

In his chronicle of the Gallic war, Cæsar in each book completed the narrative
of a year's campaign. In treating of the civil war he devotes the first and second
books to the doings of one year. There are three distinct episodes of the year's
campaign narrated in the second;—the taking of Marseilles, the subjugation of the
southern province of Spain,—if that can be said to be subjugated which gave itself
up very readily,—and the destruction of a Roman army in Africa under the hands
of a barbarian king. But of all Cæsar's writings it is perhaps the least interesting, as
it tells us but little of what Cæsar did himself,—and in fact contains chiefly Cæsar's
records of the doings of his lieutenants by sea and land.

He begins by telling us of the enormous exertions made both by the besiegers
and by the besieged at Massilia, which town was now held by Domitius on the part
of Pompey,—to supplement whom at sea a certain Nasidius was sent with a large
fleet. Young Brutus, as will be remembered, was attacking the harbour on behalf
of Cæsar, and had already obtained a victory over the Massilians before Nasidius
came up; and Trebonius, also on the part of Cæsar, was besieging the town from
the land. This Decimus Brutus was one of those conspirators who afterwards conspired against Cæsar and slew him,—and Trebonius was another of the number.
The wise Greeks of the city,—more wise than fortunate, however,—had explained
to Cæsar when he first expressed his wish to have the town on his side, that really
to them there was no difference between Pompey and Cæsar, both of whom they
loved with all their hearts,—but they had been compelled to become partisans of
Pompey, the Pompeian general Domitius being the first to enter their town; and
now they find themselves obliged to fight as Pompeians in defence of their wealth
and their homes. Thus driven by necessity, they fight well and do their very best to
favour the side which we must henceforward call that of the Republic as against an
autocrat;—for, during this siege of Marseilles, Cæsar had been appointed Dictator,
and a law to that effect had been passed at Rome, where the passing of such a law
was no doubt easy enough in the absence of Pompey, of the consuls, and of all the
senators who were Pompey's friends.

The Massilians had now chosen their side, and they do their very best. We
are told that the Cæsarean troops, from the high ground on which Trebonius had
placed his camp, could look down into the town, and could see "how all the youth
who had been left in the city, and all the elders with their children and wives, and
the sentinels of the city, either stretched their hands to heaven from the walls, or,

entering the temples of the immortal gods, and throwing themselves before their sacred images, prayed that the heavenly powers would give them victory. Nor was there one among them who did not believe that on the result of that day depended all that they had,"—namely, liberty, property, and life; for the Massilians, doubtless, had heard of Avaricum, of Alesia, and of Uxellodunum. "When the battle was begun," says Cæsar, "the Massilians failed not at all in valour; but, mindful of the lessons they had just received from their townsmen, fought with the belief that the present was their only opportunity of doing aught for their own preservation; and that to those who should fall in battle, loss of life would only come a little sooner than to the others, who would have to undergo the same fate, should the city be taken." Cæsar, as he wrote this, doubtless thought of what he had done in Gaul when policy demanded from him an extremity of cruelty; and, so writing, he enhanced the clemency with which, as he is about to tell us, he afterwards treated the Massilians. When the time came it did not suit him to depopulate a rich town, the trade of whose merchants was beneficial both to Rome and to the Province. He is about to tell us of his mercy, and therefore explains to us beforehand how little was mercy expected from him. We feel that every line he writes is weighed, though the time for such weighing must have been very short with one whose hands were so full as were always the hands of Cæsar.

Nasidius, whom we may call Pompey's admiral, was of no use at all. The Massilians, tempted by his coming, attack bravely the ship which bears the flag of young Brutus; but young Brutus is too quick for them, and the unhappy Massilians run two of their biggest vessels against each other in their endeavour to pin that of the Cæsarean admiral between them. The Massilian fleet is utterly dispersed. Five are sunk, four are taken: one gets off with Nasidius, who runs away, making no effort to fight; who has been sent there,—so Cæsar hints,—by Pompey, not to give assistance, but only to pretend to give assistance. One ship gets back into the harbour with the sad tidings; and the Massilians—despairing only for a moment at the first blush of the bad news—determine that their walls may still be defended.

The town was very well supplied with such things as were needed for defence, the people being a provident people, well instructed and civilised, with means at their command. We are told of great poles twelve feet long, with sharp iron heads to them, which the besiegers could throw with such force from the engines on their walls as to drive them through four tiers of the wicker crates or stationary shields which the Cæsareans built up for their protection,—believing that no force could drive a weapon through them. As we read of this we cannot but think of Armstrong and Whitfield guns, and iron plates, and granite batteries, and earthworks. These terrible darts, thrown from "balistæ," are very sore upon the Cæsareans; they therefore contrive an immense tower, so high that it cannot be reached by any weapon, so built that no wood or material subject to fire shall be on the outside,—which they erect story by story, of very great strength. And as they raise this step by step, each story is secured against fire and against the enemy. The reader,—probably not an engineer himself,—is disposed to think as he struggles through this minute description of the erection which Cæsar gives, and endeavours to realise the way in which it is done, that Cæsar must himself have served specially as an engineer. But in truth he was not at this siege himself, and had nothing to do with the planning of the tower, and must in this instance at least have got a written description from his officer,—as he probably did before when he built the memorable bridge over the Rhine. And when the tower is finished, they make a long covered way or shed,—musculum or muscle Cæsar calls it; and with this they form for themselves a passage from the big tower to a special point in the walls of the town. This muscle is so strong with its sloping roof that nothing thrown upon it will break or burn it. The Massilians try tubs of flaming pitch, and great fragments of rock; but these simply slip to the ground, and are pulled away with long poles and forks. And the Cæsareans, from the height of their great tower, have so terrible an advantage! The Massilians cannot defend their wall, and a breach is made, or almost made.

The Massilians can do no more. The very gods are against them. So they put on the habit of supplicants, and go forth to the conquerors. They will give their city to Cæsar. Cæsar is expected. Will Trebonius be so good as to wait till Cæsar comes? If Trebonius should proceed with his work so that the soldiers should absolutely get into the town, then;—Trebonius knows very well what would happen then. A little delay cannot hurt. Nothing shall be done till Cæsar comes. As it happens, Cæsar has already especially ordered that the city shall be spared; and a kind of truce is made, to endure till Cæsar shall come and take possession. Trebonius has a difficulty in keeping his soldiers from the plunder; but he does restrain them, and besiegers and besieged are at rest, and wait for Cæsar.

But these Massilians are a crafty people. The Cæsarean soldiers, having agreed to wait, take it easily, and simply amuse themselves in these days of waiting. When they are quite off their guard, and a high wind favours the scheme, the Massilians rush out and succeed in burning the tower, and the muscle, and the rampart, and the sheds, and all the implements. Even though the tower was built with brick, it burns freely,—so great is the wind. Then Trebonius goes to work, and does it all again. Because there is no more wood left round about the camp, he makes a rampart of a new kind,—hitherto unheard of,—with bricks. Doubtless the Cæsarean soldiers had first to make the bricks, and we can imagine what were their feelings in reference to the Massilians. But however that may be, they work so well and so hard that the Massilians soon see that their late success is of no avail. Nothing is left to them. Neither perfidy nor valour can avail them, and now again they give themselves up. They are starved and suffering from pestilence, their fortifications are destroyed, they have no hope of aid from without,—and now they give themselves up,—intending no fraud. "Sese dedere sine fraude constituunt." Domitius, the Pompeian general, manages to escape in a ship. He starts with three ships, but the one in which he himself sails alone escapes the hands of "young" Brutus. Surely now will Marseilles be treated with worse treatment than that which fell on the Gaulish cities. But such is by no means Cæsar's will. Cæsar takes their public treasure and their ships, and reminding them that he spares them rather for their name and old character than for any merits of theirs shown towards him, leaves two legions among them, and goes to Rome. At Avaricum, when the Gauls had fought to defend their own liberties, he had destroyed everybody;—at Alesia he had decreed the death of every inhabitant when they had simply asked him leave to pass through his camp;—at Uxellodunum he had cut off the hands and poked out the eyes of Gauls who had dared to fight for their country. But the Gauls were barbarians whom it was necessary that Cæsar should pacify. The Massilians were Greeks, and a civilised people,—and might be useful.

Before coming on to Marseilles there had been a little more for Cæsar to do in Spain, where, as was told in the last chapter, he had just compelled Afranius and Petreius to lay down their arms and disband their legions. Joined with them had been a third Pompeian general, one Varro,—a distinguished man, though not, perhaps, a great general,—of whom Cæsar tells us that with his Roman policy he veered between Pompeian and Cæsarean tactics till, unfortunately for himself, he declared for Pompey and the wrong side, when he heard that Afranius was having his own way in the neighbourhood of Lerida. But Varro is in the south of Spain, in Andalusia,—or Bætica, as it was then called,—and in this southern province of Spain it seems that Cæsar's cause was more popular than that of Pompey. Cæsar, at any rate, has but little difficulty with Varro. The Pompeian officer is deserted by his legions, and gives himself up very quickly. Cæsar does not care to tell us what he did with Varro, but we know that he treated his brother Roman with the utmost courtesy. Varro was a very learned man, and a friend of Cicero's, and one who wrote books, and was a credit to Rome as a man of letters if not as a general. We are told that he wrote 490 volumes, and that he lived to be eighty-eight,—a fate very uncommon with Romans who meddled with public affairs in these days. Cæsar made everything smooth in the south of Spain, restoring the money and treasures which Varro had taken from the towns, and giving thanks to everybody. Then he went on over the Pyrenees to Marseilles, and made things smooth there.

But in the mean time things were not at all smooth in Africa. The name of Africa was at this time given to a small province belonging to the Republic, lying to the east of Numidia, in which Carthage had stood when Carthage was a city, containing that promontory which juts out towards Sicily, and having Utica as its Roman capital. It has been already said that when Cæsar determined to gain possession of certain provinces of the Republic before he followed Pompey across the Adriatic, he sent a lieutenant with three legions into Sicily, desiring him to go on to Africa as soon as things should have been arranged in the island after the Cæsarean fashion. The Sicilian matter is not very troublesome, as Cato, the virtuous man, in whose hands the government of the island had been intrusted on behalf of the Republic, leaves it on the arrival of the Cæsarean legions, complaining bitterly of Pompey's conduct. Then Cæsar's lieutenant goes over to Africa with two legions, as commanded, proposing to his army the expulsion of one Attius Varus, who had, according to Cæsar's story, taken irregular possession of the province, keeping it on behalf of Pompey, but not allowing the governor appointed by the Republic so much as to put his foot on the shore. This lieutenant was a great favourite of Cæsar, by name Curio, who had been elected tribune of the people just when the Senate was making its attempt to recall Cæsar from his command in Gaul. In that emergency, Curio as tribune had been of service to Cæsar, and Cæsar loved the young man. He was one of those who, though noble by birth, had flung themselves among the people, as Catiline had done and Clodius,—unsteady, turbulent, un-scrupulous, vicious, needy, fond of pleasure, rapacious, but well educated, brave, and clever. Cæsar himself had been such a man in his youth, and could easily forgive such faults in the character of one who, in addition to such virtues as have been named, possessed that farther and greater virtue of loving Cæsar. Cæsar ex-pected great things from Curio, and trusted him thoroughly. Curio, with many ships and his two legions, lands in Africa, and prepares to win the province for his great friend. He does obtain some little advantage, so that he is called "Imperator" by his soldiers,—a name not given to a general till he has been victorious in the field; but it seems clear, from Cæsar's telling of the story, that Curio's own officers and own soldiers distrusted him, and were doubtful whether they would follow him, or would take possession of the ships and return to Sicily;—or would go over to Attius Varus, who had been their commander in Italy before they had deserted from Pompey to Cæsar. A council of war is held, and there is much doubt. It is not only or chiefly of Attius Varus, their Roman enemy, that they are afraid; but there is Juba in their neighbourhood, the king of Numidia, who will certainly fight for Varus and against Curio. He is Pompey's declared friend, and equally declared as Cæsar's foe. He has, too, special grounds of quarrel against Curio himself; and if he comes in person with his army,—bringing such an army as he can bring if he pleases,—it will certainly go badly with Curio, should Curio be distant from his camp. Then Curio, not content with his council of war, and anxious that his sol-diers should support him in his desire to fight, makes a speech to the legionaries. We must remember, of course, that Cæsar gives us the words of this speech, and that Cæsar must himself have put the words together.

It is begun in the third person. He,—that is Curio,—tells the men how useful they were to Cæsar at Corfinium, the town at which they went over from Pompey to Cæsar. But in the second sentence he breaks into the first person and puts the very words into Curio's mouth. "For you and your services," he says, "were cop-ied by all the towns; nor is it without cause that Cæsar thinks kindly of you, and the Pompeians unkindly. For Pompey, having lost no battle, but driven by the result of your deed, fled from Italy. Me, whom Cæsar holds most dear, and Sicily and Africa without which he cannot hold Rome and Italy, Cæsar has intrusted to your honour. There are some who advise you to desert me,—for what can be more desirable to such men than that they at the same time should circumvent me, and fasten upon you a foul crime?... But you,—have you not heard of the things done by Cæsar in Spain,—two armies beaten, two generals conquered, two provinces gained, and all this done in forty days from that on which Cæsar first saw his enemy? Can those who, uninjured, were unable to stand against him, resist him now that they are conquered? And you, who followed Cæsar when victory on his side was uncertain, now that fortune has declared herself, will you go over to the conquered side when you are about to realise the reward of your zeal?... But perhaps, though you love Cæsar, you distrust me. I will not say much of my own deserts towards you,—which are indeed less as yet than I had wished or you had expected." Then, having thus declared that he will not speak of himself, he does venture to say a few words on the subject. "But why should I pass over my own work, and the result that has been as yet achieved, and my own fortune in war?

Is it displeasing to you that I brought over the whole army, safe, without losing a ship? That, as I came, at my first onslaught, I should have dispersed the fleet of the enemy? That, in two days, I should have been twice victorious with my cavalry; that I should have cut out two hundred transports from the enemy's harbour; that I should have so harassed the enemy that neither by land nor sea could they get food to supply their wants? Will it please you to repudiate such fortune and such guidance, and to connect yourself with the disgrace at Corfinium, the flight from Italy,"—namely, Pompey's flight to Dyrrachium,—"the surrender of Spain, and the evils of this African war? I indeed have wished to be called Cæsar's soldier, and you have called me your Imperator. If it repents you of having done so, I give you back the compliment. Give me back my own name, lest it seem that in scorn you have called me by that title of honour."

This is very spirited; and the merely rhetorical assertion by Cæsar that Curio thus spoke to his soldiers is in itself interesting, as showing us the way in which the legionaries were treated by their commanders, and in which the greatest general, of that or of any age, thought it natural that a leader should address his troops. It is of value, also, as showing the difficulty of keeping any legion true to either side in a civil war, in which, on either side, the men must fight for a commander they had learned to respect, and against a commander they respected,—the commander in each case being a Roman Imperator. Curio, too, as we know, was a man who on such an occasion could use words. But that he used the words here put into his mouth, or any words like them, is very improbable. Cæsar was anxious to make the best apology he could for the gallant young friend who had perished in his cause, and has shown his love by making the man he loved memorable to all posterity.

But before the dark hour comes upon him the young man has a gleam of success, which, had he really spoken the words put into his mouth by Cæsar, would have seemed to justify them. He attacks the army of his fellow-Roman, Varus, and beats it, driving it back into Utica. He then resolves to besiege the town, and Cæsar implies that he would have been successful through the Cæsarean sympathies of the townsmen,—had it not been for the approach of the terrible Juba. Then comes a rumour which reaches Curio,—and which reaches Varus too inside the town,— that the Numidian king is hurrying to the scene with all his forces. He has finished another affair that he had on hand, and can now look to his Roman friends,— and to his Roman enemies. Juba craftily sends forward his præfect, or lieutenant, Sabura, with a small force of cavalry, and Curio is led to imagine that Juba has not come, and that Sabura has been sent with scanty aid to the relief of Varus. Surely he can give a good account of Sabura and that small body of Numidian horsemen. We see from the very first that Curio is doomed. Cæsar, in a few touching words, makes his apology. "The young man's youth had much to do with it, and his high spirit; his former success, too, and his own faith in his own good fortune." There is no word of reproach. Curio makes another speech to his soldiers. "Hasten to your prey," he says, "hasten to your glory!" They do hasten,—after such a fashion that when the foremost of them reach Sabura's troops, the hindermost of them are scattered far back on the road. They are cut to pieces by Juba. Curio is invited by one of his officers to escape back to his tent. But Cæsar tells us that Curio in that last moment replied that having lost the army with which Cæsar had trusted him, he would never again look Cæsar in the face. That he did say some such words as these, and that they were repeated by that officer to Cæsar, is probable enough. "So, fighting, he is slain;" —and there is an end of the man whom Cæsar loved.

What then happened was very sad for a Roman army. Many hurry down to the ships at the sea; but there is so much terror, so much confusion, and things are so badly done, that but very few get over to Sicily. The remainder endeavour to give themselves up to Varus; after doing which, could they have done it, their position would not have been very bad. A Roman surrendering to a Roman would, at the worst, but find that he was compelled to change his party. But Juba comes up and claims them as his prey, and Varus does not dare to oppose the barbarian king. Juba kills the most of them, but sends a few, whom he thinks may serve his purpose and add to his glory, back to his own kingdom. In doing which Juba behaved no worse than Cæsar habitually behaved in Gaul; but Cæsar always writes as though not only a Roman must regard a Roman as more than a man, but as though also all others must so regard Romans. And by making such assertions in their own behalf, Romans were so regarded. We are then told that the barbarian king of Numidia rode into Utica triumphant, with Roman senators in his train; and the names of two special Roman senators Cæsar sends down to posterity as having been among that base number. As far as we can spare them, they shall be spared.

Of Juba the king, and of his fate, we shall hear again.

CHAPTER XI.

Third Book Of The Civil War.—Cæsar Follows Pompey Into Illyria.—
The Lines Of Petra And The Battle Of Pharsalia.—B.C. 48.

Cæsar begins the last book of his last Commentary by telling us that this was
the year in which he, Cæsar, was by the law permitted to name a consul. He names
Publius Servilius to act in conjunction with himself. The meaning of this is, that,
as Cæsar had been created Dictator, Pompey having taken with him into Illyria
the consuls of the previous year, Cæsar was now the only magistrate under whose
authority a consul could be elected. No doubt he did choose the man, but the
election was supposed to have been made in accordance with the forms of the Republic. He remained at Rome as Dictator for eleven days, during which he made
various laws, of which the chief object was to lessen the insecurity caused by the
disruption of the ordinary course of things; and then he went down to Brindisi on
the track of Pompey. He had twelve legions with him, but was but badly off for
ships in which to transport them; and he owns that the health of the men is bad,
an autumn in the south of Italy having been very severe on men accustomed to
the healthy climate of Gaul and the north of Spain. Pompey, he tells us, had had a
whole year to prepare his army,—a whole year, without warfare, and had collected men and ships and money, and all that support which assent gives, from Asia
and the Cyclades, from Corcyra, Athens, Bithynia, Cilicia, Phœnicia, Egypt, and
the free states of Achaia. He had with him nine Roman legions, and is expecting
two more with his father-in-law Scipio out of Syria. He has three thousand archers
from Crete, from Sparta, and from Pontus; he has twelve hundred slingers, and
he has seven thousand cavalry from Galatia, Cappadocia, and Thrace. A valorous
prince from Macedonia had brought him two hundred men, all mounted. Five
hundred of Galatian and German cavalry, who had been left to overawe Ptolemy
in Egypt, are brought to Pompey by the filial care of young Cnæus. He too had
armed eight hundred of their own family retainers, and had brought them armed.
Antiochus of Commagena sends him two hundred mounted archers,—mercenar-
ies, however, not sent without promise of high payment. Dardani,—men from
the land of old Troy, Bessi, from the banks of the Hebrus, Thessalians and Mace-
donians, have all been crowded together under Pompey's standard. We feel that
Cæsar's mouth waters as he recounts them. But we feel also that he is preparing
for the triumphant record in which he is about to tell us that all these swarms did
he scatter to the winds of heaven with the handful of Roman legionaries which he
at last succeeded in landing on the shores of Illyria.

Pompey has also collected from all parts "frumenti vim maximam"—"a great power of corn indeed," as an Irishman would say, translating the words literally. And he has covered the seas with his ships, so as to hinder Cæsar from coming out of Italy. He has eight vice-admirals to command his various fleets,—all of whom Cæsar names; and over them all, as admiral-in-chief, is Bibulus, who was joint-consul with Cæsar before Cæsar went to Gaul, and who was so harassed during his consulship by the Cæsareans that he shut himself up in his house, and allowed Cæsar to rule as sole consul. Now he is about to take his revenge; but the vengeance of such a one as Bibulus cannot reach Cæsar.

Cæsar having led his legions to Brindisi, makes them a speech which almost beats in impudence anything that he ever said or did. He tells them that as they have now nearly finished all his work for him;—they have only got to lay low the Republic with Pompey the Great, and all the forces of the Republic—to which, however, have to be added King Ptolemy in Egypt, King Pharnaces in Asia, and King Juba in Numidia;—they had better leave behind them at Brindisi all their little property, the spoils of former wars, so that they may pack the tighter in the boats in which he means to send them across to Illyria,—if only they can escape the mercies of ex-Consul Admiral Bibulus. There is no suggestion that at any future time they will recover their property. For their future hopes they are to trust entirely to Cæsar's generosity. With one shout they declare their readiness to obey him. He takes over seven legions, escaping the dangers of those "rocks of evil fame," the Acroceraunia of which Horace tells us,—and escaping Bibulus also, who seems to have shut himself up in his ship as he did before in his house during the consulship. Cæsar seems to have made the passage with the conviction that had he fallen into the hands of Bibulus everything would have been lost. And with ordinary precaution and diligence on the part of Bibulus such would have been the result. Yet he makes the attempt,—trusting to the Fortune of Cæsar,—and he succeeds. He lands at a place which he calls Palæste on the coast of Epirus, considerably to the south of Dyrrachium, in Illyria. At Dyrrachium Pompey had landed the year before, and there is now stored that wealth of provision of which Cæsar has spoken. But Bibulus at last determines to be active, and he does manage to fall upon the empty vessels which Cæsar sends back to fetch the remainder of his army. "Having come upon thirty of them, he falls upon them with all the wrath occasioned by his own want of circumspection and grief, and burns them. And in the same fire he kills the sailors and the masters of the vessels,—hoping to deter others," Cæsar tells us, "by the severity of the punishment." After that we are not sorry to hear that he potters about on the seas very busy, but still incapable, and that he dies, as it seems, of a broken heart. He does indeed catch one ship afterwards,—not laden with soldiers, but coming on a private venture, with children, servants, and suchlike, dependants and followers of Cæsar's camp. All these, including the children, Bibulus slaughters, down to the smallest child. We have, however, to remember that the story is told by Cæsar, and that Cæsar did not love Bibulus.

Marc Antony has been left at Brindisi in command of the legions which Cæsar could not bring across at his first trip for want of sufficient ship-room, and is pressed very much by Cæsar to make the passage. There are attempts at treaties made, but as we read the account we feel that Cæsar is only obtaining the delay which is necessary to him till he shall have been joined by Antony. We are told how by this time the camps of Cæsar and Pompey have been brought so near together that they are separated only by the river Apsus,—for Cæsar had moved northwards towards Pompey's stronghold. And the soldiers talked together across the stream; "nor, the while, was any weapon thrown,—by compact between those who talked." Then Cæsar sends Vatinius, as his ambassador, down to the river to talk of peace; and Vatinius demands with a loud voice "whether it should not be allowed to citizens to send legates to citizens, to treat of peace;—a thing that has been allowed even to deserters from the wilds of the Pyrenees and to robbers,—especially with so excellent an object as that of hindering citizens from fighting with citizens." This seems so reasonable, that a day is named, and Labienus,—who has deserted from Cæsar and become Pompeian,—comes to treat on one side of the river, and Vatinius on the other. But,—so Cæsar tells the story himself,—the Cæsarean soldiers throw their weapons at their old general. They probably cannot endure the voice or sight of one whom they regard as a renegade. Labienus escapes under the protection of those who are with him,—but he is full of wrath against Cæsar. "After this," says he, "let us cease to speak of treaties, for there can be no peace for us till Cæsar's head has been brought to us." But the colloquies over the little stream no doubt answered Cæsar's purpose.

Cæsar is very anxious to get his legions over from Italy, and even scolds Antony for not bringing them. There is a story,—which he does not tell himself,—that he put himself into a small boat, intending to cross over to Brindisi in a storm, to hurry matters, and that he encouraged the awe-struck master of the boat by reminding him that he would carry "Cæsar and his fortunes." The story goes on to say that the sailors attempted the trip, but were driven back by the tempest.

At last there springs up a south-west wind, and Antony ventures with his flotilla,—although the war-ships of Pompey still hold the sea, and guard the Illyrian coast. But Cæsar's general is successful, and the second half of the Cæsarean army is carried northward by favouring breezes towards the shore in the very sight of Pompey and his soldiers at Dyrrachium. Two ships, however, lag behind and fall into the hands of one Otacilius, an officer belonging to Pompey. The two ships, one full of recruits and the other of veterans, agree to surrender, Otacilius having sworn that he will not hurt the men. "Here you may see," says Cæsar, "how much safety to men there is in presence of mind." The recruits do as they have undertaken, and give themselves up;—whereupon Otacilius, altogether disregarding his oath, like a true Roman, kills every man of them. But the veterans, disregarding their word also, and knowing no doubt to a fraction the worth of the word of Otacilius, run their ship ashore in the night, and, with much fighting, get safe to Antony. Cæsar implies that the recruits even would have known better had they not been sea-sick; but that even bilge-water and bad weather combined had failed to touch the ancient courage of the veteran legionaries. They were still good men—"item conflictati et tempestatis et sentinæ vitiis."

We are then told how Metellus Scipio, coming out of Syria with his legions into Macedonia, almost succeeds in robbing the temple of Diana of Ephesus on his way. He gets together a body of senators, who are to give evidence that he counts the money fairly as he takes it out of the temple. But letters come from Pompey just as he is in the act, and he does not dare to delay his journey even to complete so pleasant a transaction. He comes to meet Pompey and to share his command at the great battle that must soon be fought. We hear, too, how Cæsar sends his lieutenants into Thessaly and Ætolia and Macedonia, to try what friends he has there, to take cities, and to get food. He is now in a land which has seemed specially to belong to Pompey; but even here they have heard of Cæsar, and the Greeks are simply anxious to be friends with the strongest Roman of the day. They have to judge which will win, and to adhere to him. For the poor Greeks there is much difficulty in forming a judgment. Presently we shall see the way in which Cæsar gives a lesson on that subject to the citizens of Gomphi. In the mean time he joins his own forces to those lately brought by Antony out of Italy, and resolves that he will force Pompey to a fight.

We may divide the remainder of this last book of the second Commentary into two episodes, — the first being the story of what occurred within the lines at Petra, and the second the account of the crowning battle of Pharsalia. In the first Pompey was the victor, — but the victory, great as it was, has won from the world very little notice. In the second, as all the world knows, Cæsar was triumphant and henceforward dominant. And yet the affair at Petra should have made a Pharsalia unnecessary, and indeed impossible. Two reasons have conspired to make Pompey's complete success at Petra unimportant in the world's esteem. This Commentary was written not by Pompey but by Cæsar; and then, unfortunately for Pompey, Pharsalia was allowed to follow Petra.

It is not very easy to unravel Cæsar's story of the doings of the two armies at Petra. Nor, were this ever so easy, would our limits or the purport of this little volume allow us to attempt to give that narrative in full to our readers. Cæsar had managed to join the legions which he had himself brought from Italy with those which had crossed afterwards with Antony, and was now anxious for a battle. His men, though fewer in number than they who followed Pompey, were fit for fighting, and knew all the work of soldiering. Pompey's men were for the most part beginners; — but they were learning, and every week added to their experience was a week in Pompey's favour. With hope of forcing a battle, Cæsar managed to get his army between Dyrrachium, in which were kept all Pompey's stores and wealth of war, and the army of his opponent, so that Pompey, as regarded any approach by land, was shut off from Dyrrachium. But the sea was open to him. His fleet was everywhere on the coast, while Cæsar had not a ship that could dare to show its bow upon the waters.

There was a steep rocky promontory some few miles north of Dyrrachium, from whence there was easy access to the sea, called Petra, or the rock. At this point Pompey could touch the sea, but between Petra and Dyrrachium Cæsar held the country. Here, on this rock, taking in for the use of his army a certain somewhat wide amount of pasturage at the foot of the rock, Pompey placed his army, and made intrenchments all round from sea to sea, fortifying himself, as all Roman generals knew how to do, with a bank and ditch and twenty-four turrets and earthworks that would make the place absolutely impregnable. The length of his lines was fifteen Roman miles,—more than thirteen English miles,—so that within his works he might have as much space as possible to give him grass for his horses. So placed, he had all the world at his back to feed him. Not only could he get at that wealth of stores which he had amassed at Dyrrachium, and which were safe from Cæsar, but the coasts of Greece, and Asia, and Egypt were open to his ships. Two things only were wanting to him,—sufficient grass for his horses, and water. But all things were wanting to Cæsar,—except grass and water. The Illyrian country at his back was one so unproductive, being rough and mountainous, that the inhabitants themselves were in ordinary times fed upon imported corn. And Pompey, foreseeing something of what might happen, had taken care to empty the storehouses and to leave the towns behind him destitute and impoverished.

Nevertheless Cæsar, having got the body of his enemy, as it were, imprisoned at Petra, was determined to keep his prisoner fast. So round and in front of Pompey's lines he also made other lines, from sea to sea. He began by erecting turrets and placing small detachments on the little hills outside Pompey's lines, so as to prevent his enemy from getting the grass. Then he joined these towers by lines, and in this way surrounded the other lines,—thinking that so Pompey would not be able to send out his horsemen for forage; and again, that the horses inside at Petra might gradually be starved; and again "that the reputation,"—"auctoritatem,"—"which in the estimation of foreign nations belonged chiefly to Pompey in this war, would be lessened when the story should have been told over the world that Pompey had been besieged by Cæsar, and did not dare to fight."

We are, perhaps, too much disposed to think,—reading our history somewhat cursorily,—that Cæsar at this time was everybody, and that Pompey was hardly worthy to be his foe. Such passages in the Commentary as that above translated,—they are not many, but a few suffice,—show that this idea is erroneous. Up to this period in their joint courses Pompey had been the greater man; Cæsar had done very much, but Pompey had done more—and now he had on his side almost all that was wealthy and respectable in Rome. He led the Conservative party, and was still confident that he had only to bide his time, and that Cæsar must fall before him. Cæsar and the Cæsareans were to him as the spirits of the Revolution were in France to Louis XVI., to Charles X., and to Louis-Philippe, before they had made their powers credible and formidable; as the Reform Bill and Catholic Emancipation were to such men as George IV. and Lord Eldon, while yet they could be opposed and postponed. It was impossible to Pompey that the sweepings of Rome, even with Cæsar and Cæsar's army to help them, should at last prevail over himself and over the Roman Senate. "He was said at that time," we are again translating Cæsar's words, "to have declared with boasts among his own people, that he would not himself deny that as a general he should be considered to be worthless if Cæsar's legions should now extricate themselves from the position in which they had rashly entangled themselves without very great loss"—"maximo detrimento"—loss that should amount wellnigh to destruction. And he was all but right in what he said.

There was a great deal of fighting for the plots of grass and different bits of vantage-ground,—fighting which must have taken place almost entirely between the two lines. But Cæsar suffered under this disadvantage, that his works, being much the longest, required the greatest number of men to erect them and prolong them and keep them in order; whereas Pompey, who in this respect had the least to do, having the inner line, was provided with much the greater number of men to do it. Cæsar's men, being veterans, had always the advantage in the actual fighting; but in the mean time Pompey's untried soldiers were obtaining that experience which was so much needed by them. Nevertheless Pompey suffered very much. They could not get water on the rock, and when he attempted to sink wells, Cæsar so perverted the water-courses that the wells gave no water. Cæsar tells us that he even dammed up the streams, making little lakes to hold it, so that it should not trickle down in its underground courses to the comfort of his enemies; but we should have thought that any reservoirs so made must soon have overflown themselves, and have been useless for the intended purpose. In the mean time Cæsar's men had no bread but what was made of a certain wild cabbage,—"chara,"—which grew there, which they kneaded up with milk, and lived upon it cheerfully, though it was not very palatable. To show the Pompeians the sort of fare with which real veterans could be content to break their fasts, they threw loaves of this composition across the lines; for they were close together, and could talk to each other, and the Pompeians did not hesitate to twit their enemies with their want of provisions. But the Cæsareans had plenty of water,—and plenty of meat; and they assure Cæsar that they would rather eat the bark off the trees than allow the Pompeians to escape them.

But there was always this for Cæsar to fear,—that Pompey should land a detachment behind his lines and attack him at the back. To hinder this Cæsar made another intrenchment, with ditch and bank, running at right angles from the shore, and was intending to join this to his main work by a transverse line of fortifications running along that short portion of the coast which lay between his first lines and the second, when there came upon him the disaster which nearly destroyed him. While he was digging his trenches and building his turrets the fighting was so frequent that, as Cæsar tells us, on one day there were six battles. Pompey lost two thousand legionaries, while Cæsar lost no more than twenty; but every Cæsarean engaged in a certain turret was wounded, and four officers lost their eyes. Cæsar estimates that thirty thousand arrows were thrown upon the men defending this tower, and tells us of one Scæva, an officer, who had two hundred and thirty holes made by these arrows in his own shield.[12] We can only surmise that it must have

[12] Dean Merivale in his account of this affair reduces the number of holes in Scæva's shield to one hundred and twenty,—on the joint authority, no doubt, of Florus and Valerius Maximus; but Florus lived 200 and Val. Max. 300 years after Cæsar. Suetonius allows the full number of holes, but implies that 120 were received while the warrior was fighting in one place, and 110 while fighting in another. Lucan sings the story of Scæva at great length, but does not give the number of wounds in the shield. He seems to say that Scæva was killed on this occasion, but is not quite clear on the point. That Scæva had one eye knocked out is certain. Lucan does indeed tell us, in the very last lines of his poem, that in Egypt Cæsar once again saw his beloved centurion;—but at the moment described even Cæsar was dismayed, and the commentators doubt whether it was not Scæva's ghost that Cæsar then saw. Valerius Maximus is sure that Scæva was killed when he got the wounds;—but,

been a very big shield, and that there must have been much trouble in counting the holes. Cæsar, however, was so much pleased that he gave Scæva a large sum of money,—something over £500, and, allowing him to skip over six intermediate ranks, made him at once first centurion—or Primipilus of the legion. We remember no other record of such quick promotion—in prose. There is, indeed, the well-known case of a common sailor who did a gallant action and was made first-lieutenant on the spot; but that is told in verse, and the common sailor was a lady.

Two perfidious Gauls to whom Cæsar had been very kind, but whom he had been obliged to check on account of certain gross peculations of which they had been guilty, though, as he tells us, he had not time to punish them, went over to Pompey, and told Pompey all the secrets of Cæsar's ditches, and forts, and mounds,—finished and unfinished. Before that, Cæsar assures us, not a single man of his had gone over to the enemy, though many of the enemy had come to him. But those perfidious Gauls did a world of mischief. Pompey, hearing how far Cæsar was from having his works along the sea-shore finished, got together a huge fleet of boats, and succeeded at night in throwing a large body of his men ashore between Cæsar's two lines, thus dividing Cæsar's forces, and coming upon them in their weakest point. Cæsar admits that there was a panic in his lines, and that the slaughter of his men was very great. It seems that the very size of his own works produced the ruin which befel them, for the different parts of them were divided one from another, so that the men in one position could not succour those in another. The affair ended in the total rout of the Cæsarean army. Cæsar actually fled, and had Pompey followed him we must suppose that then there would have been an end of Cæsar. He acknowledges that in the two battles fought on that day he lost 960 legionaries, 32 officers, and 32 standards.

And then Cæsar tells us a story of Labienus, who had been his most trusted lieutenant in the Gallic wars, but who had now gone over to Pompey, not choosing to fight against the Republic. Labienus demanded of Pompey the Cæsarean captives, and caused them all to be slaughtered, asking them with scorn whether veterans such as they were accustomed to run away. Cæsar is very angry with Labienus; but Labienus might have defended himself by saying that the slaughter of prisoners of war was a custom he had learned in Gaul. As for those words of scorn, Cæsar could hardly have heard them with his own ears, and we can understand that he should take delight in saying a hard thing of Labienus.

Pompey was at once proclaimed Imperator. And Pompey used the name, though the victory had, alas! been gained over his fellow-countrymen. "So great was the effect of all this on the spirits and confidence of the Pompeians, that they thought no more of the carrying on of the war, but only of the victory they had gained." And then Cæsar throws scorn upon the Pompeians, making his own apology in the same words. "They did not care to remember that the small number of our soldiers was the cause of their triumph, or that the unevenness of the ground and narrowness of the defiles had aught to do with it; or the occupation of our lines, and the panic of our men between their double fortifications; or our

if so, how could he have been rewarded and promoted? The matter has been very much disputed; but here it has been thought best to adhere to Cæsar.

army cut into two parts, so that one part could not help the other. Nor did they add to this the fact that our men, pressed as they were, could not engage themselves in a fair conflict, and that they indeed suffered more from their own numbers, and from the narrowness of the ravines, than from the enemy. Nor were the ordinary chances of war brought to mind,—how small matters, such as some unfounded suspicion, a sudden panic, a remembered superstition, may create great misfortune; nor how often the fault of a general, or the mistake of an officer, may bring injury upon an army. But they spread abroad the report of the victory of that day throughout all the world, sending forth letters and tales as though they had conquered solely by their own valour, nor was it possible that there should after this be a reverse of their circumstances." Such was the affair of Petra, by which the relative position in the world-history of Cæsar and Pompey was very nearly made the reverse of what it is.

Cæsar now acknowledges that he is driven to change the whole plan of his campaign. He addresses a speech to his men, and explains to them that this defeat, like that at Gergovia, may lead to their future success. The victory at Alesia had sprung from the defeat of Gergovia, because the Gauls had been induced to fight; and from the reverses endured within the lines of Petra might come the same fortune;—for surely now the army of Pompey would not fear a battle. Some few officers he punishes and degrades. His own words respecting his army after their defeat are very touching. "So great a grief had come from this disaster upon the whole army, and so strong a desire of repairing its disgrace, that no one now desired the place of tribune or centurion in his legion; and all, by way of self-imposed punishment, subjected themselves to increased toil; and every man burned with a desire to fight. Some from the higher ranks were so stirred by Cæsar's speech, that they thought that they should stand their ground where they were, and fight where they stood." But Cæsar was too good a general for that. He moves on towards the south-east, and in retreating gets the better of Pompey, who follows him with only half a heart. After a short while Pompey gives up the pursuit. His father-in-law, Scipio, has brought a great army from the east, and is in Thessaly. As we read this we cannot fail to remember how short a time since it was that Cæsar himself was Pompey's father-in-law, and that Pompey was Cæsar's friend because, with too uxorious a love, he clung to Julia, his young wife. Pompey now goes eastward to unite his army to that of Scipio; and Cæsar, making his way also into Thessaly by a more southern route, joins certain forces under his lieutenant Calvinus, who had been watching Scipio, and who barely escaped falling into Pompey's hands before he could reach Cæsar. But wherever Fortune or Chance could interfere, the Gods were always kind to Cæsar.

Then Cæsar tells us of his treatment of two towns in Thessaly, Gomphi and Metropolis. Unluckily for the poor Gomphians, Cæsar reaches Gomphi first. Now the fame of Pompey's victory at Petra had been spread abroad; and the Gomphians, who,—to give them their due,—would have been just as willing to favour Cæsar as Pompey, and who only wanted to be on the winning side that they might hold their little own in safety, believed that things were going badly with Cæsar. They therefore shut their gates against Cæsar, and sent off messengers to Pompey. They can hold their town against Cæsar for a little while, but Pompey must come quickly to their aid. Pompey comes by no means quick enough, and the Gomphians' capacity to hold their own is very short-lived. At about three o'clock in the afternoon Cæsar begins to besiege the town, and before sunset he has taken it, and given it to be sacked by his soldiers. The men of Metropolis were also going to shut their gates, but luckily they hear just in time what had happened at Gomphi,—and open them instead. Whereupon Cæsar showers protection upon Metropolis; and all the other towns of Thessaly, hearing what had been done, learn what Cæsar's favour means.

Pompey, having joined his army to that of Scipio, shares all his honours with his father-in-law. When we hear this we know that Pompey's position was not comfortable, and that he was under constraint. He was a man who would share his honour with no one unless driven to do so. And indeed his command at present was not a pleasant one. It was much for a Roman commander to have with him the Roman Senate,—but the senators so placed would be apt to be less obedient than trained soldiers. They even accuse him of keeping them in Thessaly because he likes to lord it over such followers. But they were, nevertheless, all certain that Cæsar was about to be destroyed; and, even in Pompey's camp, they quarrel over the rewards of victory which they think that they will enjoy at Rome when their oligarchy shall have been re-established by Pompey's arms.

Before the great day arrives Labienus again appears on the scene; and Cæsar puts into his mouth a speech which he of course intends us to compare with the result of the coming battle. "Do not think, O Pompey, that this is the army which conquered Gaul and Germany,"—where Labienus himself was second in command under Cæsar. "I was present at all those battles, and speak of a thing which I know. A very small part of that army remains. Many have perished,—as a matter of course in so many battles. The autumn pestilence killed many in Italy. Many have gone home. Many have been left on the other shore. Have you not heard from our own friends who remained behind sick, that these cohorts of Cæsar's were made up at Brindisi?"—made up but the other day, Labienus implies. "This army, indeed, has been renewed from levies in the two Gauls; but all that it had of strength perished in those two battles at Dyrrachium;"—in the contests, that is, within the lines of Petra. Upon this Labienus swears that he will not sleep under canvas again until he sleeps as victor over Cæsar; and Pompey swears the same, and everybody swears. Then they all go away full of the coming victory. We daresay there was a great deal of false confidence; but as for the words which Cæsar puts into the mouth of Labienus, we know well how much cause Cæsar had to dislike Labienus, and we doubt whether they were ever spoken.

At length the battle-field is chosen,—near the town of Pharsalus, on the banks of the river Enipeus in Thessaly. The battle has acquired world-wide fame as that of Pharsalia, which we have been taught to regard as the name of the plain on which it was fought. Neither of these names occur in the Commentary, nor does that of the river; and the actual spot on which the great contest took place seems to be a matter of doubt even now. The ground is Turkish soil,—near to the mountains which separate modern Greece from Turkey, and is not well adapted for the researches of historical travellers. Cæsar had been keeping his men on the march close to Pompey, till Pompey found that he could no longer abstain from fighting. Then came Labienus with his vaunts, and his oath,—and at length the day and the field were chosen. Cæsar at any rate was ready. At this time Cæsar was fifty-two years old, and Pompey was five years his elder.

Cæsar tells us that Pompey had 110 cohorts, or eleven legions. Had the legions been full, Pompey's army would have contained 66,000 legionaries; but Cæsar states their number at 45,000, or something over two-thirds of the full number. He does not forget to tell us once again that among these eleven were the two legions which he had given up in obedience to the demand of the Senate. Pompey himself, with these two very legions, placed himself on the left away from the river; and there also were all his auxiliaries,—not counted with the legionaries,—slingers, archers, and cavalry. Scipio commanded in the centre with the legions he had brought out of Syria. So Cæsar tells us. "We learn from other sources that Lentulus commanded Pompey's right wing, lying on the river—and Domitius, whom we remember as trying to hold Marseilles against young Brutus and Trebonius, the left. Cæsar had 80 cohorts, or eight legions, which should have numbered 48,000 men had his legions been full;—but, as he tells us, he led but 22,000 legionaries, so that his ranks were deficient by more than a half. As was his custom, he had his tenth legion to the right, away from the river. The ninth, terribly thinned by what had befallen it within the lines at Petra, joined to the eleventh, lay next the river, forming part of Cæsar's left wing. Antony commanded the left wing, Domitius Calvinus, whom Cæsar sometimes calls by one name and sometimes by the other, the centre,—and Sulla the right. Cæsar placed himself to the right, with his tenth legion, opposite to Pompey. As far as we can learn, there was but little in the nature of the ground to aid either of them;—and so the fight began.

There is not much complication, and perhaps no great interest, in the account of the actual battle as it is given by Cæsar. Cæsar makes a speech to his army, which was, as we have already learned, and as he tells us now, the accustomed thing to do. No falser speech was ever made by man, if he spoke the words which he himself reports. He first of all reminds them how they themselves are witnesses that he has done his best to insure peace;—and then he calls to their memory certain mock treaties as to peace, in which, when seeking delay, he had pretended to engage himself and his enemy. He had never wasted, he told them, the blood of his soldiers, nor did he desire to deprive the Republic of either army—"alterutro exercitu"—of Pompey's army or of his own. They were both Roman, and far be it from him to destroy aught belonging to the Republic. We must acknowledge that Cæsar was always chary of Roman life and Roman blood. He would spare it when it could be spared; but he could spill it like water when the spilling of it was necessary to his end. He was very politic; but as for tenderness,—neither he nor any Roman knew what it was.

Then there is a story of one Crastinus, who declares that whether dead or alive he will please Cæsar. He throws the first weapon against the enemy and does please Cæsar. But he has to please by his death, for he is killed in his effort.

Pompey orders that his first rank shall not leave its order to advance, but shall receive the shock of Cæsar's attack. Cæsar points out to us that he is wrong in this, because the very excitement of a first attack gives increased energy and strength to the men. Cæsar's legionaries are told to attack, and they rush over the space intervening between the first ranks to do so. But they are so well trained that they pause and catch their breath before they throw their weapons. Then they throw their piles and draw their swords, and the ranks of the two armies are close pitted against each other.

But Pompey had thought that he could win the battle, almost without calling on his legionaries for any exertion, by the simple strategic movement of his numerous cavalry and auxiliaries. He outnumbered Cæsar altogether, but in these arms he could overwhelm him with a cloud of horsemen and of archers. But Cæsar also had known of these clouds. He fought now as always with a triple rank of legionaries,—but behind his third rank,—or rather somewhat to their right shoulder,—he had drawn up a choice body of men picked from his third line,—a fourth line as it were,—whose business it was to stand against Pompey's clouds when the attempt should be made by these clouds upon their right flank. Cæsar's small body of cavalry did give way before the Pompeian clouds, and the horsemen and the archers and the slingers swept round upon Cæsar's flank. But they swept round upon destruction. Cæsar gave the word to that fourth line of picked men. "Illi—they," says Cæsar, "ran forward with the greatest rapidity, and with their standards in advance attacked the cavalry of Pompey with such violence that none of them could stand their ground;—so that all not only were forced from the ground, but being at once driven in panic, they sought the shelter of the highest mountains near them. And when they were thus removed, all the archers and the slingers, desolate and unarmed, without any one to take care of them, were killed in heaps." Such is Cæsar's account of Pompey's great attack of cavalry which was to win the battle without giving trouble to the legions.

Cæsar acknowledges that Pompey's legionaries drew their swords bravely and began their share of the fighting well. Then at once he tells us of the failure on the part of the cavalry and of the slaughter of the poor auxiliary slingers, and in the very next sentence gives us to understand that the battle was won. Though Pompey's legions were so much more numerous than those of Cæsar, we are told that Cæsar's third line attacked the Pompeian legionaries when they were "defessi"—worn out. The few cohorts of picked men who in such marvellous manner had dispersed Pompey's clouds, following on their success, turned the flank of Pompey's legions and carried the day. That it was all as Cæsar says there can be little doubt. That he won the battle there can, we presume, be no doubt. Pompey at once flew to his camp and endeavoured to defend it. But such defence was impossible, and Pompey was driven to seek succour in flight. He found a horse and a few companions, and did not stop till he was on the sea-shore. Then he got on board a provision-vessel, and was heard to complain that he had been betrayed by those very men from whose hands he had expected victory.

We are told with much picturesque effect how Cæsar's men, hungry, accustomed to endurance, patient in all their want, found Pompey's camp prepared for victory, and decked in luxurious preparation for the senatorial victors. Couches were strewn, and plate was put out, and tables prepared, and the tents of these happy ones were adorned with fresh ivy. The senatorial happy ones have but a bad time of it, either perishing in their flight, or escaping into the desert solitudes of the mountains. Cæsar follows up his conquest, and on the day after the battle compels the great body of the fugitives to surrender at discretion. He surrounds them on the top of a hill and shuts them out from water, and they do surrender at discretion. With stretched-out hands, prone upon the earth, these late conquerors, the cream of the Roman power, who had so lately sworn to conquer ere they slept, weeping beg for mercy. Cæsar, having said a few words to them of his clemency, gave them their lives. He recommends them to the care of his own men, and desires that they may neither be slaughtered nor robbed.

Cæsar says he lost only 200 soldiers in that battle—and among them 30 officers, all brave men. That gallant Crastinus was among the 30. Of Pompey's army 15,000 had been killed, and 24,000 had surrendered! 180 standards and 9 eagles were taken and brought to Cæsar. The numbers seem to us to be almost incredible, whether we look at those given to us in regard to the conqueror or the conquered. Cæsar's account, however, of that day's work has hitherto been taken as authoritative, and it is too late now to question it. After this fashion was the battle of Pharsalia won, and the so-called Roman Republic brought to an end.

But Cæsar by no means thought that his work was done;—nor indeed was it nearly done. It was now clearly his first duty to pursue Pompey,—whom, should he escape, the outside provinces and distant allies of the Republic would soon supply with another army. "Cæsar thought that Pompey was to be pursued to the neglecting of all other things." In the mean time Pompey, who seems to have been panic-struck by his misfortune, fled with a few friends down the Ægean Sea, picked his young wife up at an island as he went, and made his way to Egypt. The story of his murder by those who had the young King of Egypt in their keeping is well known and need not detain us. Cæsar tells it very shortly. Pompey sends to young Ptolemy for succour and assistance, trusting to past friendship between himself and the young king's father. Ptolemy is in the hands of eunuchs, adventurers, and cut-throat soldiers, and has no voice of his own in the matter. But these ruffians think it well to have Pompey out of the way, and therefore they murder him. Achillas, a royal satrap, and Septimius, a Roman soldier, go out to Pompey's vessel, as messengers from the king, and induce him to come down into their boat. Then, in the very sight of his wife, he is slaughtered, and his head is carried away as proof of the deed. Such was the end of Pompey, for whom no fortune had seemed to be too great, till Cæsar came upon the scene. We are told by the Roman poet, Lucan, who took the battle of Pharsalia as his difficult theme, that Cæsar could bear no superior, and Pompey no equal. The poet probably wished to make the latter the more magnanimous by the comparison. To us, as we examine the character of the two generals, Cæsar seems at least as jealous of power as his son-in-law, and certainly was the more successful of the two in extruding all others from a share in the power which he coveted. Pompey in the triumvirate admitted his junior to more, as he must have felt it, than equal power: Cæsar in the triumvirate simply made a stepping-stone of the great man who was his elder. Pompey at Thessaly was forced to divide at least the name of his power with Scipio, his last father-in-law: but Cæsar never gave a shred of his mantle to be worn by another soldier.

In speaking, however, of the character of Pompey, and in comparing it with that of his greater rival, it may probably be said of him that in all his contests, both military and political, he was governed by a love of old Rome, and of the Republic as the greatest national institution which the world had ever known, and by a feeling which we call patriotism, and of which Cæsar was,—perhaps, we may say, too great to be capable. Pompey desired to lead, but to lead the beloved Republic. Cæsar, caring nothing for the things of old, with no reverence for the past, utterly destitute of that tenderness for our former footsteps which makes so many of us cling with passionate fondness to convicted errors, desired to create out of the dust of the Republic,—which fate and his genius allowed him to recast as he would,—something which should be better and truer than the Republic.

The last seven chapters of the third book of this Commentary form a commencement of the record of the Alexandrine war,—which, beyond those seven chapters, Cæsar himself did not write. That he should have written any Commentary amidst the necessary toils of war, and the perhaps more pressing emergencies of his political condition, is one of the greatest marvels of human power. He tells us now, that having delayed but a few days in Asia, he followed Pompey first to Cyprus and then to Egypt, taking with him as his entire army three thousand two hundred men. "The rest, worn out with wounds, and battles, and toil, and the greatness of the journey, could not follow him." But he directed that legions should be made up for him from the remnants of Pompey's broken army, and, with a godlike trust in the obedience of absent vassals, he went on to Egypt. He tells us that he was kept in Alexandria by Etesian winds. But we know also that Cleopatra came to him at Alexandria, requiring his services in her contest for the crown of Egypt; and knowing at what price she bought them, we doubt the persistent malignity of the Etesian winds, Had Cleopatra been a swarthy Nubian, as some have portrayed her, Cæsar, we think, would have left Alexandria though the Etesian winds had blown in his very teeth. All winds filled Cæsar's sails. Cæsar gets possession of Cleopatra's brother Ptolemy, who, in accordance with their father's will, was to have reigned in conjunction with his sister, and the Alexandrians rise against him in great force. He slays Photinus, the servant of King Ptolemy, has his own ambassador slain, and burns the royal fleet of Egypt,—burning with it, unfortunately, the greater part of the royal library. "These things were the beginning of the Alexandrine war." These are the last words of Cæsar's last Commentary.

CHAPTER XII.
CONCLUSION.

Having concluded his ten short chapters descriptive of the ten books of the Commentaries written by Cæsar himself, the author of this little Volume has finished his intended task,—and as he is specially anxious not to be thought to have made an attempt at writing history, he would not add any concluding words, were it not that three other Commentaries of Cæsar's three other wars were added to Cæsar's Commentaries by other writers. There is the Commentary on the Alexandrine war,—written probably by Hirtius, the author of the last book of the Gallic war; and two Commentaries on the African war and the Spanish war,—written, as the critics seem to think, by one Oppius, a friend whom Cæsar loved and trusted. The Alexandrine war was a war of itself, in which Cæsar was involved by his matchless audacity in following Pompey into Egypt, and perhaps by the sweetness of Cleopatra's charms. And this led also to a war in Asia Minor, the account of which is included with that of his Egyptian campaign. The African war, and that afterwards carried on in Spain with the object of crushing out the sparks of Pompeian revolt against his power, are simply the latter portions of the civil war, and their records might have been written as chapters added to the Commentary "De Bello Civili."

Alexandria, when Cæsar landed there in pursuit of Pompey and had offered to him as a graceful tribute on his first arrival the head of his murdered rival, was a city almost as populous and quite as rich as Rome; and in the city, and throughout the more fertile parts of Egypt, there was a crowd of Roman soldiers left there to support and to overawe the throne of the Ptolemies. Cæsar, with hardly more than half a full legion to support him, enters Alexandria as though obedience were due to him by all in Egypt as Roman consul. He at once demands an enormous sum of money, which he claims as due to himself personally for services rendered to a former Ptolemy; he takes possession of the person of Ptolemy the young king,—and is taken possession of by Cleopatra, the young king's sister, who was joint-heir with her brother to the throne. In all his career there was perhaps nothing more audacious than his conduct in Egypt. The Alexandrians, or rather perhaps the Roman army in Egypt under the leading of the young king's satraps, rise against Cæsar, and he is compelled to fortify himself in the town. He contrives, however, to burn all the Egyptian fleet, and with it unfortunately the royal library, as we were told by himself at the end of the last Commentary. He at length allows Ptolemy to go, giving him back to the Egyptians, and thinking that the young king's presence may serve to allay the enmity of the Alexandrians. The young king wept at leaving Cæsar, and declared that even his own kingdom was not so dear to him as the companionship of Cæsar. But the crafty false-faced boy turns against Cæsar as soon as he is free to do so. Cæsar never was in greater danger; and as one reads one feels one's self to be deprived of the right to say that no more insane thing was ever done than Cæsar did when he swaggered into Alexandria without an army at his back,—only by the remembrance that Cæsar was Cæsar. First, because he wanted some ready money, and secondly, because Cleopatra was pretty, Cæsar nearly lost the world in Egypt.

But there comes to his help a barbarian ally,—a certain Mithridates of Pergamus, a putative son of the great Mithridates of Pontus. Mithridates brings an army to Cæsar's rescue, and does rescue him. A great battle is fought on the Nile,—a battle which would have been impossible to Cæsar had not Mithridates come to his aid,—and the Egyptians are utterly dispersed. Young Ptolemy is drowned; Cleopatra is settled on her throne; and Egypt becomes subject to Cæsar. Then Cæsar hurries into Asia, finding it necessary to quell the arrogance of a barbarian who had dared to defeat a Roman general. The unfortunate conqueror is Pharnaces, the undoubted son of Mithridates of Pontus. But Cæsar comes, and sees, and conquers. He engages Pharnaces at Zela, and destroys his army; and then, we are told, inscribed upon his banners those insolent words—"Veni, vidi, vici." He had already been made Dictator of the Roman Empire for an entire year, and had revelled with Cleopatra at Alexandria, and was becoming a monarch.

These were the campaigns of the year 47 B.C., and the record of them is made in the Commentary "De Bello Alexandrino."

In the mean time things have not been going altogether smoothly for Cæsar in Italy, although his friends at Rome have made him Dictator. His soldiers have mutinied against their officers, and against his authority; and a great company of Pompeians is collected in that province of Africa in which poor Curio was conquered by Juba,—when Juba had Roman senators walking in his train, and Cæsar's army was destroyed. The province called by the name of Africa lay just opposite to Sicily, and was blessed with that Roman civilisation which belonged to the possessions of the Republic which were nearest to Rome, the great centre of all things. It is now the stronghold of the Republican faction,—as being the one spot of Roman ground in which Cæsar had failed of success. Pompey, indeed, is no more, but Pompey's two sons are here,—and Scipio, Pompey's father-in-law, whom Pompey had joined with himself in the command at Pharsalus. Labienus is here, who, since he turned from Cæsar, has been more Pompeian than Pompey himself; and Afranius, to whom Cæsar was so kind in Spain; and Petreius and King Juba,—of whom a joint story has yet to be told; and Varus, who held the province against Curio;—and last of all there is that tower of strength, the great Cato, the most virtuous and impracticable of men, who, in spite of his virtue, is always in the wrong, and of whom the world at large only remembers that he was fond of wine, and that he destroyed himself at Utica.

They are all at Utica,—and to them for the present Utica is Rome. They establish a Senate; and Scipio, who is unworthy of the great name he bears, and is incompetent as a general, is made commander-in-chief, because Cato decides that law and routine so require. Scipio had been consul,—had been joint commander with Pompey,—and his rank is the highest. The same argument had been used when he was joined in that command,—that it was fitting that such power should be given to him because he was of consular rank. The command of the Republican fleet had been intrusted to Bibulus on the same ground. We never hear of Cæsar so bestowing promotion. He indeed is now and again led away by another fault, trusting men simply because he loves them,—by what we may call favouritism,—as he did when he allowed Curio to lose his army in Africa, and thus occasioned all this subsequent trouble. As we read of Scipio's rank we remember that we have heard of similar cause for ill-judged promotion in later times. The Pompeians, however, collect an enormous army. They have ten Roman legions, and are supported, moreover, by the whole force of King Juba. This army, we are told, is as numerous as that which Pompey commanded at Pharsalus. There is quarrelling among them for authority; quarrelling as to strategy; jealousy as to the barbarian, with acknowledged inability to act without him;—and the reader feels that it is all in vain. Cæsar comes, having quelled the mutiny of his own old veterans in Italy by a few words. He has gone among them fearing nothing; they demand their discharge—he grants it. They require the rewards which they think to be their due, and he tells them that they shall have their money,—when he has won it with other legions. Then he addresses them not as soldiers, but as "citizens"—"Quirites;" and that they cannot stand; it implies that they are no longer the invincible soldiers of Cæsar. They rally round him; the legions are re-formed, and he lands in Africa with a small army indeed,—at first with little more than three thousand men,—and is again nearly destroyed in the very first battle. But after a few months campaigning the old story has to be told again. A great battle is fought at Thapsus, a year and five months after that of Pharsalia, and the Republic is routed again and for ever. The commentator tells us that on this occasion the ferocity of Cæsar's veterans was so great, that by no entreaties, by no commands, could they be induced to cease from the spilling of blood.

But of the destruction of the leaders separate stories are told us. Of Cato is the first story, and that best known to history. He finds himself obliged to surrender the town of Utica to Cæsar; and then, "he himself having carefully settled his own affairs, and having commended his children to Lucius Cæsar, who was then acting with him as his quæstor, with his usual gait and countenance, so as to cause no suspicion, he took his sword with him into his bedroom when it was his time to retire to rest,—and so killed himself." Scipio also killed himself. Afranius was killed by Cæsar's soldiers. Labienus, and the two sons of Pompey, and Varus, escaped into Spain. Then comes the story of King Juba and Petreius. Juba had collected his wives and children, and all his wealth of gold and jewels and rich apparel, into a town of his called Zama; and there he had built a vast funeral-pile, on which, in the event of his being conquered by Cæsar, he intended to perish,—meaning that his wives and children and dependants and rich treasures should all be burned with him. So, when he was defeated, he returned to Zama; but his wives and children and dependants, being less magnificently minded than their king, and knowing his royal purpose, and being unwilling to become ornaments to his euthanasia, would not let him enter the place. Then he went to his old Roman friend Petreius, and they two sat down together to supper. Petreius was he who would not allow Afranius to surrender to Cæsar at Lerida. When they have supped, Juba proposes that they shall fight each other, so that one at least may die gloriously. They do fight, and Petreius is quickly killed. "Juba being the stronger, easily destroyed the weaker Petreius with his sword." Then the barbarian tried to kill himself; but, failing, got a slave to finish the work. The battle of Thapsus was fought, B.C. 47. Numidia is made a province by Cæsar, and so Africa is won. We may say that the Roman Republic died with Cato at Utica.

The Spanish war, which afforded matter for the last Commentary, is a mere stamping out of the embers. Cæsar, after the affair in Africa, goes to Rome; and the historian begins his chronicle by telling us that he is detained there "muneribus dandis,"—by the distribution of rewards,—keeping his promise, no doubt, to those veterans whom he won back to their military obedience by calling them "Quirites," or Roman citizens.[13] The sons of Pompey, Cnæus and Sextus, have collected together a great number of men to support their worn-out cause, and we are told that in the battle of Munda more than 30,000 men perished. But that was the end of it. Labienus and Varus are killed; and the historian tells us that a funeral was made for them. One Scapula, of whom it is said that he was the promoter of all this Spanish rebellion, eats his supper, has himself anointed, and is killed on his funeral-pile. Cnæus, the elder son of Pompey, escapes wounded, but at last is caught in a cave, and is killed. Sextus, the younger, escapes, and becomes a leading rebel for some years longer, till at last he also is killed by one of Antony's officers.

This Commentary is ended, or rather is brought to an untimely close, in the middle of a speech which Cæsar makes to the inhabitants of Hipsala,—Seville,—in which he tells them in strong language how well he behaves to them, and how very badly they have behaved to him. But we reach an abrupt termination in the middle of a sentence.

After the battle of Munda Cæsar returned to Rome, and enjoyed one year of magnificent splendour and regal power in Rome. He is made Consul for ten years, and Dictator for life. He is still high priest, and at last is called King. He makes many laws, and perhaps adds the crowning jewel to his imperishable diadem of glory by reforming the calendar, and establishing a proper rotation of months and days, so as to comprise a properly-divided year. But as there is no Commentary of this year of Cæsar's life, our readers will not expect that we should treat of it here. How he was struck to death by Brutus, Cassius, and the other conspirators, and fell at the foot of Pompey's statue, gathering his garments around him gracefully, with a policy that was glorious and persistent to the last, is known to all men and women.

---

[13] Not in the Commentary, but elsewhere, we learn that he now triumphed four times, for four different victories, taking care to claim none for any victory won over Roman soldiers. On four different days he was carried through the city with his legions and his spoils and his captives. His first triumph was for the Gallic wars; and on that day Vercingetorix, the gallant Gaul whom we remember, and who had now been six years in prison, was strangled to do Cæsar honour. I think we hate Cæsar the more for his cruelty to those who were not Romans, because policy induced him to spare his countrymen.

> "Then burst his mighty heart;
> And in his mantle muffling up his face,
> Even at the base of Pompey's statua,
> Which all the while ran blood, Great Cæsar fell."

That he had done his work, and that he died in time to save his name and fame from the evil deeds of which unlimited power in the State would too probably have caused the tyrant to be guilty, was perhaps not the least fortunate circumstance in a career which for good fortune has been unequalled in history.

THE END.

Lector House believes that a society develops through a two-fold approach of continuous learning and adaptation, which is derived from the study of classic literary works spread across the historic timeline of literature records. Therefore, we aim at reviving, repairing and redeveloping all those inaccessible or damaged but historically as well as culturally important literature across subjects so that the future generations may have an opportunity to study and learn from past works to embark upon a journey of creating a better future.

This book is a result of an effort made by Lector House towards making a contribution to the preservation and repair of original ancient works which might hold historical significance to the approach of continuous learning across subjects.

HAPPY READING & LEARNING!

LECTOR HOUSE LLP
E-MAIL: lectorpublishing@gmail.com

www.ingramcontent.com/pod-product-compliance
Lightning Source LLC
Chambersburg PA
CBHW031209160726
47992CB00006B/2643